The World of the
SOUTHERN INDIANS

The World of the SOUTHERN INDIANS

Virginia Pounds Brown
Laurella Owens

Illustrations by Nathan H. Glick

NewSouth Books
Montgomery | Louisville

NewSouth Books
105 S. Court Street
Montgomery, AL 36104

Publishing history: This book was originally published in 1983 by
Beechwood Books, Leeds, Alabama, with the ISBN 0-912221-
06-2. The book was reprinted at least six times by Beechwood
before the present NewSouth edition. The current edition closely
follows the original design by Bob and Faith Nance but was
retypeset and the pages recomposed digitally for modern printing
methods.

Library of Congress Cataloging-in-Publication Data

Brown, Virginia Pounds.
The world of the southern Indians / Virginia Pounds Brown,
Laurella Owens ; illustrations by Nathan H. Glick.
p. cm.
"Originally published in 1983 by Beechwood Books, Leeds, Alabama."
Includes bibliographical references and index.

ISBN-13: 978-1-58838-252-8
ISBN-10: 1-58838-252-4

1. Indians of North America—Southern States—Juvenile
literature. I. Owens, Laurella. II. Glick, Nathan H. (Nathan
Harold), 1912- ill. III. Title.
E78.S65B76 2010
975'.01—dc22

2010048323

Printed in the United States of America by Sheridan Books

Contents

For Bestor

Preface

This book has been written in response to a need expressed particularly by librarians and teachers for a basic book about Indians of the South. It is intended not only for students but also for anyone with a curiosity about the Indians. We have tried to be simple and direct and to present the material in an interesting way with many illustrations. Our role has been to bring together widely scattered information on Southern Indians.

The main focus is on the five great tribes in the South—how they lived, where they lived, what happened to them. In a section on the states of the area—Alabama, Florida, Georgia, Mississippi, North Carolina, South Carolina, and Tennessee—we have located places where Indian history can be seen.

There is no doubt that the Southern Indians have been neglected. From television, movies, and books we know more about the Western Indians than we do about the Indians who lived in the South. The words of Chief Joseph of the Nez Perce, as he surrendered his tribe to United States authority, ring in our ears. But no less moving and equally eloquent is the little-known speech, fifty years earlier, of the Creek chief Speckled Snake in response to white claims on Indian land in the South.

Why have we white Southerners been reluctant to pursue

our Indian heritage? Could it be that we wished not only to remove the Indians bodily from the South but also to erase their very existence from our memory? Be that as it may, we seem now at last to be more willing to look at and to study about these people with whom we share a common heritage—the South.

Over the years in which this book has been prepared we have been helped by many people: Elizabeth Beamguard, Elloie Bradshaw, John Egerton, John Fletcher, Virginia Hamilton, Frances Henckell, Pat Howron, Betty Hurtt, Mary Bess Kirksey, Ed MacMahon, Jim and Ruth Manasco, Margaret Miller, Herman Moore, Pat Moore, Margaret Robertson, Donette Sparks, Gene Thomas, Iva Jewel Tucker, Marvin Whiting, Pearl Wilson, Martha Wood, W.G. Woolfolk, Eva Yates.

We are particularly indebted to the following for their reading of the manuscript and their suggestions: Linda McNair Cohen, James Seay Brown, W. Stuart Harris, Tom Hendrix, Jacqueline A. Matte, Jane McRae, Lindy Martin.

The World of the

SOUTHERN INDIANS

SHAWNEES

TENNESSEE

CHICKASAWS

YUCHIS

KOASATIS

CHEROKEES

TUSCARORAS

NORTH CAROLINA

CATAWBAS

SOUTH CAROLINA

YAMASEES

ALABAMA

CREEKS

MISSISSIPPI

ALIBAMOS

GUALES

GEORGIA

CHOCTAWS

NATCHEZ

APALACHEES

TIMUCUAS

FLORIDA

CALUSAS

Introduction

Indians
of the
South

Although the Indians lived in the South long before any other peoples, we speak of their history as spanning three centuries. That history began in the early 1500s, when Spanish explorers traveled through the area, and ended about 1840, after most of the Southern Indians had been moved west of the Mississippi. These "historic" years are the years for which we have written records.

The years before the sixteenth century are called "prehistoric." We can guess what the Indians of earlier times were like from what we dig up or pick up, like burial urns, weapon points or pottery, and from what we see on the landscape, like mounds. We also have clues from customs and ceremonies that were carried on by the later Indians.

At the time the first Spanish explorers arrived (1513), more Indians were living in the South than in any other part of the continent except Mexico. The Indians had been attracted to the area because of excellent living conditions. The climate was mild, with much rain. Forests provided deer and rabbit and other animals to eat, and numerous rivers and lakes yielded many kinds of fish. Around the rivers rich soil waited to be tilled. So the Indians settled down to plant crops and build towns. In time they enjoyed a civilized life that, in North America, was second only to that of the Indians of Mexico.

Who were the people the first white explorers found? They included the Calusas [kah-LOO-suz], the Timucuas [tim-uh-KOO-uz], and the Apalachees of Florida. Also there were the Guales [WAH-leez] and the Yamasees [YΛ-muh-seez] of Georgia and South Carolina. To the west there were the Natchez [NATCH-ee] of the lower Mississippi River Valley. Within a short time, many of these tribal names disappeared. Why did this happen? When the white men met the Indians they sometimes killed them or took them captive. Also, when the Indians associated with the whites they often caught diseases from which they had no immunity, like smallpox, and died. The greatest damage caused by the meeting of the Indians and the whites was the upsetting of the harmonious relationship with the natural world that was so important to the Indian way of life. For example, in contrast to earlier times when they had hunted only for the needs of the tribe of clan, the Indians now hunted to have pelts to exchange for European trinkets or "fire water," as they called the white man's whiskey.

Tribes of the South as we know them (except for the Seminoles) had become definite groupings by around A.D. 1700. It is not easy to label them, because Southern tribes more than any other North American tribes tended to merge, then separate, and some to die out. But these are the main tribes and their locations:

- the Cherokees in west North Carolina, north Georgia, east Tennessee, and northeast Alabama;
- the Chickasaws in the corners where Tennessee, Mississippi, and Alabama meet;
- the Choctaws in southwest Alabama and central and south Mississippi;
- the Creeks in Alabama and Georgia;
- and the Seminoles in Florida.

The story of each of these tribes—how they lived, who their leaders were, how they got along with the white people—is told in this book in the section given the tribal name.

It is impossible to write of the Indians of any one state without writing at the same time about the Indians of neighboring states. Indian tribes lived all over the South, certain tribes in certain areas, long before the United States Government created state boundaries. For example, both Chickasaw and Choctaw tribal lands extended into west Alabama but their main holdings were in Mississippi. To understand the Indians in the South we have to cross state lines for the good reason that for the Indians such boundaries never existed.

Indians of the South spoke several languages. Muskogean was the dominant language, spoken by Choctaws, Chickasaws, Creeks, and Seminoles.

The Iroquoian language was represented by the Cherokees and the Tuscaroras. The Catawbas of the Carolinas spoke Siouan [SOO-un]. The Yuchis [YOO-cheez] spoke a language unrelated to any other.

Most of the Indians did not call themselves by their tribal names. They called themselves simply "the people," "the first men," "the principal people," or "the original people." Most tribal names were given to them by other Indians or whites as a means of identification. Frequently the name indicated where they lived or how they lived. The Chickasaws were named by the Choctaws, the tribe from whom they broke away. *Chik-asha* comes from the phrase meaning "they left as a tribe not a very great while ago." One tribe that was called by its self-chosen name was the Yuchis; the name means "children of the sun."

The term "Five Civilized Tribes" refers to the Cherokees, Chickasaws, Choctaws, Creeks, and Seminoles. The term was used by white people after these tribes moved to Oklahoma. Their "civilized" ways, such as farming and self-government, stood in sharp contrast to the life of the "wild" Plains Indians also living in Oklahoma.

The descendants of those Indians who left their homes in the South in the 1830s live today, for the most part, in Oklahoma. Some of the tribespeople managed to remain in their Southern homeland; their descendants, now proud to claim their Indian names, are working hard to preserve their cultural heritage.

The Long Story of the Southern Indians

ICE AGE	PALEO-INDIAN PERIOD	ARCHAIC PERIOD	WOODLAND PERIOD

Between 100,000 B.C. and 10,000 B.C	**10,000 B.C. to 8000 B.C. (about 12,000 years ago)**	**8000 B.C. to 1000 B.C. (about 10,000 years ago)**	**1000 B.C. to A.D. 700 (about 3,000 years ago)**
Glaciers cover top half of North America	Ice Age ends	People gather nuts, seeds, shellfish; and hunt deer and other small game	Begin growing gourds, corn (maize), squash
Asians cross land bridge to North America	Hunters use traps and stone-dripped spears to kill large animals	Atlatl (spear-thrower) used in hunting	Begin using bow and arrow
Hunters follow large animals to east and south US	Cutting and scraping tools are made of stone	Begin making pottery	Weave rough cloth and use cord and fiber in making pottery
			Build burial mounds
			Make ornaments of copper, stone, lead, and freshwater pearls

What Was Happening at the Same Time in the Rest of the World

Ice Age people live in caves in Spain and France	People of Asia and Europe are also using stone implements	**Pyramids of Egypt built** **Shang dynasty, China, in power** Stonehenge, England, built	Jesus Christ born Olympic Games begin in Greece Buddha born

MISSISSIPPIAN PERIOD	BEGINNING OF HISTORIC PERIOD	HISTORIC PERIOD	REMOVAL TO WEST	RENEWAL IN THE SOUTH
A.D. 700 to 1500 (about 1,000 years ago)	1500 to 1700 (about 500 years ago)	1700 to 1830	1820-1840 1840 to present	1980s
Build large earthen mounds with buildings on top Chiefs head towns and villages Use simple hoes and plows in farming Fish from dugout canoes Make fine pottery; and jewelry from stones, bones, shells	Reach height of a rich and complex culture Meet white people from Europe who enter their lands	Five great tribes—Choctaws, Chickasaws, Cherokees, Creeks, and Seminoles face the whites—and lose their lands	Removed by US Government to Indian Territory in Arkansas and Oklahoma Tribes begin again in the West	Communities of Indians living in the South reclaim their heritage
Toltecs dominate Yucatan William the Conqueror invades England Mongols invade China	Cortes invades Mexico Pilgrims land on Plymouth Rock Taj Mahal, India, built	French Revolution Captain James Cook visits Northwest United States becomes a nation		

Ice Age hunters close in for the kill. As ice melted and grass appeared, prehistoric animals drifted into the Tennessee Valley to graze. Pictured here is a mastodon, ancestor of the elephant.

1

They Discovered the South

Prehistoric Indians

Hiking along a creek bank after a rain, your foot kicks up a small stone that catches your eye because its shape and markings tell you here is something made by human hands. Finding that small stone may be your first link with the people of prehistoric times in the South. By "prehistoric" we mean the period before written records were made, that is, before about A.D. 1500.

Other parts of the landscape around you may hide more prehistoric treasures. A dark shadow behind the trees at the base of a cliff suggests a cave which may have been a shelter for hunters or a home for several families in Archaic or Paleo-Indian times. Buried under or washed away by a lakefront or river edge may be shell ornaments and pottery fragments from a village or camp of the Woodland era. A few hundred yards from the field where you play ball you may notice an overgrown mound that seems different from a natural hill; possibly it is the remains of one of the earthen heaps built by the Mound Builders who lived about eight hundred years ago.

Most of these traces of very early Indian life are either buried or lost. And the objects that have been found are too difficult for the untrained person to interpret. But archaeologists (specialists in the study of remains of long-ago life) have learned much about prehistoric Indians from these relics.

They have written books about what they have learned and have set up exhibits in museum, which help us know more about these early peoples.

The ancestors of the Indians who lived in the South came to this continent more than 20,000 years ago, traveling from northwestern Asia. They may have come over a land bridge that does not exist today. The land bridge, between what is now Siberia and Alaska, was created when the seas sank from supplying huge amounts of moisture for the ice masses that covered much of North America. Some researchers believe that the first people crossed over the ice after the land bridge disappeared under the sea.

The Asiatic immigrants did not come all at once. A steady stream of people crossed slowly into Alaska and, perhaps, followed the valleys southward along the eastern ridge of the Rock Mountains and into the plains. Gradually, traveling in small bands and pursuing huge animals like bison and mammoths, the early Americans moved eastward into the area that later became the southern United States.

The first people who came to the South arrived during the last Ice Age. In the ten thousand years between that time and the coming of the white men about A.D. 1500, early man went through four stages of development. We call those stages, or periods of time, the Paleo-Indian period, the Archaic period, the Woodland period, and the Mississippian period. The follow pages tell more about these early peoples.

During the Ice Age a steady, slow stream of people crossed from Asia into Alaska over the Bering Strait, using a land bridge that does not exist today. Gradually traveling in bands and pursuing prehistoric animals, some groups moved southeastward to become the first Southerners.

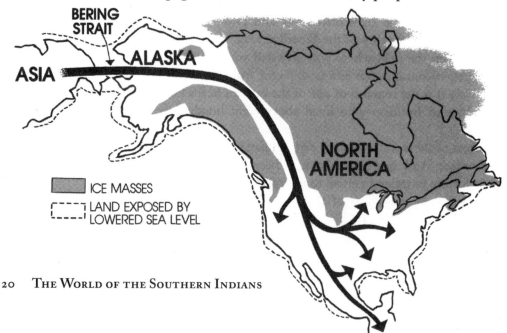

BERING STRAIT

ALASKA

ASIA

NORTH AMERICA

ICE MASSES

LAND EXPOSED BY LOWERED SEA LEVEL

Hunters (*Paleo-Indian Period*)

The first Southerners we know about lived in the Paleo [PAY-le-oh]-Indian period, which began about 12,00 years ago (10,000 B.C.). They hunted large, now-extinct animals such as the mammoth, an elephant-like creature. Paleo-Indian people also ate smaller animals and plants.

The early hunters stayed on the move, because they were always looking for food. They lived in small bands of about twenty-five people. Men did the hunting and made the stone tools and weapons. Women took care of the children, gathered firewood and plants for food, made clothes out of animal skins, and did the cooking.

Paleo-Indians used pieces of hard stone to strike or scrape bits of chert (a form of quartz) until they achieved the spear-tip shape they wanted. They refined the basic shape by flaking the point with pieces of deer antler. Sometimes a flute, or groove, was made by striking the base of the point with a specially shaped piece of deer antler, thereby removing a channel flake down its center. The flute made the projectile point fit snugly against the wood spear when it was tied on tightly with strips of animal hide. (See "How Early Man Hunted," p.22.)

A group of hunters would wait for animals to come to drink at a lakeside or by a stream; then they would move cautiously closer and attack quickly, aiming the spears at the animals' ribs. The hunters used almost every part of the animal they killed. Besides the flesh, which was roasted or dried for eating, the skin was used for clothing and containers, the tendons for wrapping, and the bones for scrapers and others tools.

Archaeologists have discovered some of the ancient campsites of the early hunters and have found several types of early spear points. Clovis points (named for a place in New Mexico where the first one was found) have been found at the Quad site near Decatur, Alabama, and at a dig site near Macon, Georgia.

How Early Man Hunted

Early man made weapons because he had to kill animals for food. His survival depended on his ability to hunt fresh meat. For a long time—many thousands of years—he did not know how to grow vegetables or preserve food. But all around him were wild animals, and he gradually learned how best to kill them and prepare them for eating and for many other uses: clothes, bone tools, rope, skin shelters.

1. In the earliest method of hunting, man threw pointed sticks and stones at animals, or jabbed them with these weapons, to wound and kill them.

2. Then, the hunter learned to tie sharp stones, or points, to sticks to make spears and darts. He developed skill in breaking stone to get sharp edges for cutting or gouging. The stone tips are called projectile points.* (*Projectile* [pro-JECK-tul] means something thrown.) The type of point called the Redstone (shown here) was sometimes as large as 4 1/2 inches long. The fluting, or groove hollowed out down the center of the blade, allowed it to be snugly tied to the spear.

3. The early hunter's next great improvement in weaponry was the atlatl [AT-ul-LAT-ul], which allowed the hunter of the Archaic period to throw with great force and to keep at a safe distance from animals. The atlatl was a piece of wood two or three feet long, with a small based carved into one end. A weight was tied on to give added power. The hunter held the spear resting on the atlatl and against the notched end; then he lifted the atlatl

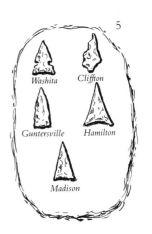

Washita

Cliffton

Guntersville

Hamilton

Madison

over his shoulder and, with a whiplike motion, sent the spear hurtling toward the target.

4. Hunters of the South learned to make and use the bow and arrow about 1500 B.C. The bow acted as a spring, releasing a lot of power all at once. As power behind projectiles increased, the size of shafts and points became smaller. (The bow was invented in the Old World about 5,000 years ago, and later came to eastern North America.)

5. Tiny and delicate, the stone points used by hunters of the Mississippian period were well suited to killing small game with bows and arrows. They are sometimes called bird points.

The Southern Indians had no firearms until the Europeans brought guns, about A.D. 1500.

---

*A stone implement is also called a point, although it served as a knife and not as the tip on a spear or dart. An expert using a microscope can often tell whether a point was used as a knife; certain wear marks show on it. If a stone tool was used as a scraper this too can be determined by studying he edge with a microscope. The wear marks left by scraping are different from those left by cutting.

"Projectile point" is a better term than "arrowhead" because Southern man did not begin using the bow and arrow until about 1500 B.C.

Hints about collecting points: Because prehistoric man made his weapons and tool tips of stone—and stone lasts a long time—we who live thousands of years later can know something of what early Indian life was like. Look for points after a rain along riverbanks or when a field or new road is being bulldozed. Be careful to mark each piece, using black India ink, as to where you found it.

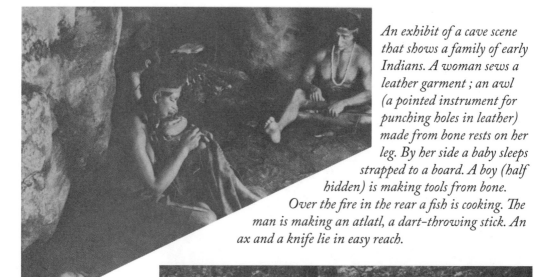

An exhibit of a cave scene that shows a family of early Indians. A woman sews a leather garment ; an awl (a pointed instrument for punching holes in leather) made from bone rests on her leg. By her side a baby sleeps strapped to a board. A boy (half hidden) is making tools from bone. Over the fire in the rear a fish is cooking. The man is making an atlatl, a dart-throwing stick. An ax and a knife lie in easy reach.

Entrance to Russell Cave, man's oldest known home in the South.

Gatherers (*Archaic Period*)

When the large animals became scarce, the early Southerners hunted smaller game like deer and rabbits and birds. This period, from about 8000 B.C. to 2000 B.C., is called the Archaic. The Archaic people also hunted with stone-tipped spears, but they added to the spear's power and accuracy by using a spear-thrower called the atlatl (see "How Early Man Hunted," p. 22).

These people settled down a bit. Their homes at first were caves or rock shelters. Later, especially during the warm spring and summer months, they built campsites near streams or near the coast where they found abundant supplies of mussels and fish, oysters and clams. Today we can still see mounds of their discarded shells. For example, on Stallings Island near Augusta, Georgia, stands an enormous mound more than 300 feet long and 300 feet wide, made up of shells from mussels and clams. In Alabama's northern counties, in the middle Tennessee Valley, are many shell pile remains.

Archaic people had a well-rounded diet. Besides fish, it included wild plant foods like hickory nuts, greens, fruits, and berries. These people also ate both fresh and dried animal meat. They dried the flesh of deer, buffalo, and smaller animals on racks in the sun.

By grinding and polishing one piece of stone with another, Archaic people added new kinds and shapes of tools. Bone was also used for tools. Other new skills learned during this period were weaving and fiber-tempered pottery. The Archaic people also made necklaces, bracelets, and beads from shells, stone, and bone.

Farmers (*Woodland Period*)

In time the hunters and gatherers learned that they could plant seeds and care for the growing plants so that they would have additional food sources. This period of the beginnings of farming was the Woodland period, 2000 B.C. to A.D.

Contrasted with corn grown today, the first corn grown in the South was tiny, no more than one inch long. It flourished with cultivation and became the staple food of the Southern Indians.

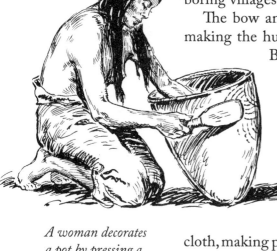

800. The early farmers grew mostly gourds, squash, and a primitive kind of corn. Their villages were larger and more permanent than those of earlier times. Although tribes had not yet been formed, the village groups began sharing their hunting and gathering grounds with each other; sometimes farmlands were also shared. These contacts between neighboring villages were the beginning of tribal life.

The bow and arrow were introduced during this time, making the hunting of deer and other game much easier. Because the bow (made of animal tendons) could propel the arrow so much harder and faster than the human arm could hurl the spear or dart, hunters no longer needed large, heavy stone points and now made smaller stone points.

Now that people had learned to store food, and could usually depend on their crops, they had time to spend on weaving cloth, making pottery, and fashioning ornaments and art objects. They had begun trading with Indians of other regions; they used conch shells from the Gulf Coast, copper and lead from the Great Lakes region, and the upper Mississippi Valley, grizzly bear teeth from the Rocky Mountains. They became skilled in dance and music and developed religious ceremonies around the planting and harvesting of corn.

A woman decorates a pot by pressing a wooden paddle, on which a design has been carved, into the wet clay pot. A more settled life gave Woodland people time to make decorated pottery as well as ornaments and art objects.

Ceremonies related to death and burials also became important. From early times, family members were buried in a shallow hole in the floor of the house. Families lived over their ancestors. With each burial the floor rose higher. During the Woodland period the Indians began building high burial mounds; the first such mounds were built about 1000 B.C. In one kind of mound, earth was piled on top of the place where a person was buried; later another body was buried and a pile of dirt was added on top. This was repeated until a large mound had been built.

To accompany the person's soul to heaven, appropriate items were placed in the grave. A warrior or hunter was buried with weapons, a farmer with agricultural tools, a woman with implements for household work. Pottery, often decorated with designs of birds or snakes, was put in the graves. Excavated mounds at Crystal River, Florida, and other burial mounds have yielded decorated pottery, smoking pipes, jewelry, and copper collars and pendants.

Mound Builders *(Mississippian Period)*

The last of the prehistoric Indians were the Mound Builders, or the people, of the Mississippian period, which lasted from about A.D. 800 to 1500. These people lived in towns or large villages and were headed by chiefs and priests.

The flat-topped, pyramid-sided mounds—which can still be seen throughout the South, especially in river valleys—differed from the burial mounds of earlier times. The new style of mounds served as foundations for temples or chiefs' houses or other important buildings. Some of the mounds were 70 or 80 feet high with bases covering several acres. At Moundville, Alabama, today can be seen what remains of the South's largest mound complex. Forty mounds stand impressively on 305 acres of flat land beside the Warrior River. A stairway of logs has been reconstructed on one side of the temple mound; it leads up to the temple at the top, which has also been reconstructed. The original temple was probably built of mud-daubed twigs and branches woven between upright poles that had been pounded into the earth. A fire was kept constantly burning in the temple. The people worshipped a fire-sun god who brought them good harvests from their corn crops.

Mounds were built in clusters around a large central plaza. In this flat area the people gathered for religious ceremonies, games, and other public activities. Many of the villages surrounding the mounds were quite large, with two or three hundred houses. The houses were rectangular in shape; like the temples, they were made with a framework of woven sticks and twigs covered and plastered with clay, and with thatched roofs. One or two thousand or more people lived in these communities.

This crested duck bowl is one of the most prized Indian artifacts in North America. Taken from a Moundville, Alabama, site, it was made of diorite, a hard, greenish stone found in the West. No doubt Moundville Indians traded for the stone (well-worn trading paths linked Indians over the Americas).

To protect themselves from enemies the mound builders surrounded their villages with wooden palisades—fences of stakes that were pointed at the top and set close together. Remains of such fences have been found at Moundville and at the Etowah Mounds near Rome, Georgia. Some palisades were built with complicated maze-like passageways where attackers would be trapped and killed by the defenders on the walls overhead. Wide ditches outside the palisades improved the defenses.

Farming was done in fields outside the fence. The farmers used hoes they had made from flint and shell, and maybe even simple wooden plows. Indians of this period grew improved strains of corn, squash, pumpkins, and beans. They stored surpluses in ceramic containers. Fishing in nearby rivers was done in dugout canoes.

The mound builders made fine pottery, often in animal shapes. A beautiful crested duck bowl was found at Moundville. Jewelry was made from stones, bones, and shells.

When the Spanish explorers traveled through the South, they found many of the temple mounds abandoned. Whole populations of large villages had vanished. What had happened? Although their disappearance is a mystery, some experts believe that earlier visits of Europeans had spread unfamiliar diseases which the Indians could not withstand because they had no built-up resistance; these diseases wiped out large communities. Although the Indians with whom the white people came in contact said they remembered nothing about the mound builders, they may well have been their descendants.

Today hundreds of the mounds still stand, silent reminders of the grandeur of a rich and vital culture.

Southern Indians believed in a life after death. Personal possesions were buried with the dead, like the copper ornament which has been "killed" so its spirit can accompany the spirit person.

Underway here is an archaeological dig. The site has been laid off in five-foot squares, and each bit of soil is being examined, sifted, and marked with the number of the square from which it came. In the right foreground is a prehistorical burial, with arms and legs folded tightly into the body. Inset shows another type of burial, found at Moundville, Alabama. A grown man of Mound Builder times was about 5 feet 7 inches tall. His life span was probably only 27 years.

A Temple Mound Center

Mound builders organized their towns or centers around several large mounds. The most important mound and the tallest was the temple mound, shown below. In the temple a sacred fire burned constantly, tended by priests. Priests also conducted the religious ceremonies so important to the Mound Builders. A high priest with two attending priests stands on top of the mound waiting to greet another priest who is climbing the steep steps. The standard rising above the entrance to the temple shows the sacred symbol of an open hand with an eye in it.

At right is a less important temple mound. In the building on top the dead may have been prepared for burial. Beside this mound is a grain storehouse.

On the mound at rear right stands the chief's house.

In the foreground a new mound is being built—or, more likely, an already existing mound is being added to. Indians had no beasts of burden or wheeled vehicles to help them build the

Mounds were built entirely by hand. Basketful after basketful of earth was carried to the top and dumped

mounds. The mounds were constructed over a long period of time, possibly by tens of thousands of people.

Note the river in the background, the palisaded fence surrounding the center, and the cornfields outside the fence.

Hernando De Soto gambled his own money that he would find in Florida a land as rich in gold as the lands of the Incas and the Aztecs. This portrait of De Soto was based on a picture made during his lifetime; the original painting is lost.

2

Southern Indians
Meet Their
First White Men

The first white people the Southern Indians saw were explorers from Spain. Indians on the Gulf Coast sighted strange-looking ships that brought ashore men wearing metal hats and armor. The Indians were amazed and awed by the soldiers riding horses, for they had never seen these animals before.

In the 1500s the Spanish sent many expeditions across the Atlantic, first to Mexico and Peru, and then to the territory they called Florida. (At that time "Florida" was a vast region reaching from the Atlantic coast westward to New Mexico and from the Gulf of Mexico to the North Pole.) Indians who came in contact with the white men discovered quickly that they were interested mainly in what they could take back to Europe. Usually the treasure they were looking for was gold.

The Calusas of Florida

The Calusas [kah-LOO-suz] were the first Southern Indians to meet the white man. Spanish ships sailing around the tip of Florida found it easy at first to lure the trusting natives aboard and then sail off with them. But the Calusas soon learned about the white man's trickery. When Ponce de Leon first set foot on Florida soil in 1513, eighty war canoes of the Calusas forced him to retreat after a day-long battle. When he returned eight years later, a Calusa arrow wounded him so badly that he died in Cuba a short time later.

The Calusas lived off the bounty of the sea that surrounded them and traded with other Indians in Cuba. They fished and collected shellfish and gathered wild vegetable food. Huge shell mounds mark the areas where they lived. Because their livelihood depended on the sea rather than on agricultural crops, they remained strong longer than most Indians threatened by Europeans. When the invading white men ransacked the other Indians' storehouses of corn, or burned their fields for refusing to cooperate, whole villages would be left without food for the coming winter. On the other hand, the Calusas got their food from the water, an area the white man could not violate.

The Caluses were not only good fishermen, they were expert swimmers and divers as well. When Spanish ships, laden with gold and silver from Mexico, wrecked on their coast, they dived for the sunken treasures. They used the

Florida Indians (Timucuas) greet the first white men they have ever seen with friendliness and gifts of skins and food. In 1564 Le Moyne made this drawing of a French expedition to the New World putting to shore at the mouth of the St. John's River, Florida.

gold and silver to make jewelry for themselves: necklaces, bracelets, earplugs. They also took Spanish survivors of the wrecks as captives. It is because one of the captives, who lived with the Calusas for twenty years, made records of his life with them that we know so much about the early Florida Indians.

The main Calusa village was located on a swampy island in Estero Bay, where today a 30-foot mound rises from the mango swamp. Here a powerful chief called Calos ruled over a chiefdom from Lake Okeechobee to the Keys. Chief Calos lived in a grand manner, wearing special clothing and receiving tribute from his subjects in the form of food, deerskins, and gold and silver from sunken Spanish ships. His subjects also provided him with several wives.

De Soto Explores Indian Country

Hernando De Soto was the first European to move inland to the heart of Indian country, and he brought the largest and best equipped army. When he had appeared before the King of Spain, proposing to explore Florida at his own expense, the King appointed him "governor of all Cuba and Florida." De Soto took a whole year getting ready for the voyage. When he sailed, his company included six hundred well-armed soldiers, plus slaves and servants. Twenty-four Catholic priests and monks went along to convert the Indians, called "savages" by Europeans of that day. The expedition carried 220 horses, a large herd of pigs, some mules, and a number of vicious bloodhounds to hunt and run down Indians.

In May 1539, this well-equipped army landed at Tampa Bay. The Timucua [tim-uh-KOO-ah] tribespeople were probably the first to encounter De Soto; they quickly found out that when the Spaniards did not get what they wanted, they could be very cruel, stealing grain from storehouses, burning towns and fields, even killing the Indians. (See "Important Small Tribes," p. 127.)

As he moved north through Florida and into southwest Georgia, De Soto kept asking where he could find gold. (The Spaniards had an interpreter, Juan Ortiz, who traveled with them; he had come to the New World in an earlier expedition and been captured by the Timucuas and learned their language.) Maybe in an attempt to get rid of the unwelcome visitors, Indians told the Spaniards about the province of Cofitachequi [koh-fee-tah-CHAY-kee], where, they said, precious metals would be found. The main town of the province was near present-day Augusta, Georgia, on the South Carolina side of the Savannah River.

It turned out that Cofitachequi had a woman ruler— the "Lady of Cofitachequi"—who came to welcome De Soto. Carried on a litter covered with a white cloth, she came as far as the river; then she was taken across the river to the Spaniards in a decorated dugout canoe. One of her attendants gave her a stool to sit on as she talked with De Soto. A Spanish onlooker noted that she was "brown but well-proportioned."

The Indian princess told the Spaniards that many of her

people had died or were weak from a terrible illness that had swept through the area. Historians believe this calamity was caused by diseases introduced to the Indians by earlier Spanish explorers; since the European diseases were new to the Indians, they had no resistance to them. in other places in the South, whole villages were wiped out by disease brought by the white man.

Although De Soto found no gold or silver at Cofitachequi, the people brought him other gifts: copper, mica, fresh-water pearls, tanned skins, venison, and salt.

Near the main village De Soto found the tribe's temple mound. The temple was 100 feet long and 40 feet wide, with a high roof and decoration of shells and pearls. The Spaniards were so impressed with the temple's contents—its statues, carved wooden chests, breastplates and shields—that they just helped themselves to what they liked, including 300 pounds of pearls. Leaving Cofitachequi, they took the Lady captive and headed northwest.

In May 1540 the Spaniards crossed the Blue Ridge

This old engraving shows De Soto landing at Tampa Bay. His expedition included 220 horses.

Mountains into the territory of the Cherokees. They did not stop long in the area of the corners of North Carolina and Tennessee but swung south again into what is now north Alabama.

We do not know what happened to the Lady of Cofitachequi.

De Soto in Alabama

De Soto had heard rumors of a wealthy Indian town called Coosa, and his expedition headed in its direction, toward present-day Gadsden and across the Coosa River near Talladega. Near Childersburg, on July 26, De Soto came upon the most advanced civilization he was to encounter on his four-year journey in North America. The people of the region lived prosperously and with a well-developed system of government. For twenty-five days the Spanish army stayed at Coosa, taking the Indians' food and supplies and forcing them to serve as burden bearers.

From Coosa the army traveled south to Tawasa, where Montgomery now stands. Here De Soto heard about gold at Maubila [moe-BEE-lah], the largest town of the Gulf Coast Indians. He continued his journey down the Alabama River to what is now Selma, and south toward Maubila, which probably was located between the lower Alabama and Tombigbee Rivers, north of present-day Mobile.

Entering the territory of the Maubilans, the Spanish army was met by Tuscaloosa, the giant chief of the tribe. Tuscaloosa was imposing in manner as well as size; when De Soto walked up to meet him, he stayed seated, according to one of the Spanish captains, "as if he had been a king." Tuscaloosa wore a turban and a feather cape; an attendant held over him a huge sunshade fan, decorated with a white cross on a black field.

But De Soto wanted to push on to Maubila, and he demanded that Tuscaloosa provide him 400 burden bearers. Maybe suspicious of what the Indians might plan in retaliation of his cruel treatment, De Soto arrested Tuscaloosa and forced him to travel with him. Along the way, Tuscaloosa's attendant walked beside him, still shielding him with the sunshade.

The Bloody Battle of Maubila

After marching three days with Tuscaloosa as captive, De Soto and his army reached Maubila. Leaving most of his men to set up camp, De Soto with Tuscaloosa and some of the Spanish captains approached the town. Maubila had a strong fence around it, "as high as three men," the Spanish recorder wrote. The fence was built of heavy, pointed posts driven into the ground, with smaller stakes tied to them at right angles on both sides. Every 50 feet along the wall was a tower which could hold seven or eight warriors.

Tuscaloosa, pretending that he was not a captive, invited the Spaniards into the town, and the Indians greeted the strangers with dancing and singing. The Spaniards got off their horses and went inside the gate. As soon as they entered, however, Tuscaloosa disappeared into one of the houses. De Soto angrily ordered an Indian to bring his chief out, but the Indian refused; and a Spanish captain killed the Indian with his lance. Immediately Maubila warriors, who had been hiding and waiting to make a surprise attack, swarmed out of houses and the battle began.

The Spaniards rushed to the gate on foot, not having time to mount their horses. The Indians tried to prevent them from escaping by closing the gate, but De Soto and most of his captains managed to get through.

Outside, the Spaniards were chased some distance by the Indians but rallied their forces. After three hours of fighting, the Indians retreated into the town. De Soto's men stormed the gate and the walls and broke through with their axes.

The Indians fought fiercely with clubs and bows and arrows, but they were no match for the Spaniards who were on horseback and wielding crossbows and swords. In one last desperate effort the Maubilans, including women and children, fought in the open square and from the houses and walls. When the Spaniards set fire to the houses, many Indians jumped into the flames, preferring death to captivity.

The battle lasted all day and ended at sunset. The Spaniards were victorious, but over twenty of their number were killed and almost all the rest were wounded. Although the Indians lost possibly as many as 5,000 dead, and their town was wiped out, they had succeeded in slowing down De Soto's march. The battle was the turning point in the Spanish expedition.

Toward the Mississippi

De Soto and his men rested for nearly a month. Then, although he knew he was within a hundred miles of the Gulf where his ships were waiting for him, and although his men were exhausted, he decided to press ahead. The army moved north through Choctaw country and then west into

Mississippi and the land of the Chickasaws. The Chicka-saws , always noted as fighters, cleverly avoided battle-type clashes with the Spaniards. Instead, they made many short and quick attacks on the Spanish camp, mostly at night. In these raids during the winter of 1541, the Indians killed several soldiers and many horses.

A narrator of De Soto's expedition wrote:

"On a certain night toward the end of January 1541 the north wind blew furiously, and the [Chickasaws] recognized how much this wind was in their favor. At one o'clock, there-fore, three squadrons of them crept silently within a hundred feet of the Spanish sentinels. Then their Curaca [war chief] gave instructions to sound a call to arms. This they did with many drums, fifes, shells that had been brought along for making a great noise. Then all shouted at the same time so as to throw more terror into the hearts of the Spanish. The Indians now attacked the town, swinging their burning faggots and shooting lighted arrows into the houses, which

The Battle of Maubila is portrayed in a miniature display at the Moundville (Ala.) Museum. The Indians with clubs and bows and arrows were no match for the Spaniards wielding crossbows and swords. In the left foreground an Indian priest entreats the sun god for help, while in front of him kneels a Spanish priest.

being made of straw caught fire instantly with the strong wind that was blowing. The Spaniards rushed out as quickly as possible to defend their lives, but they were unable to do battle because the strong wind was sweeping the flame and smoke back over them and thus damaging them extensively while contributing to the favor and defense of the Indians. The Indians entered the town, and with the aid of the fire did a great amount of damage, killing a large number of horses and Spaniards."

De Soto and his men spent the early spring traveling across what is now the state of Mississippi. On the bank of the Mississippi River—across from present-day Helen, Arkansas—they built barges to cross to the western side. As they worked, thousands of Indians gathered threateningly on the opposite bank.

The Spaniards discovered that these Indians who lived west of the great river were buffalo hunters rather than corn planters; this meant that the invaders were unable to raid grain bins and spent a hard and hungry winter in southern Arkansas.

The following spring, as the army moved south along the Mississippi River, De Soto fell ill and died, never having realized his dream of finding gold. His men buried him in the river but decided to keep moving westward. Discouraged by Indian attacks and lack of food, however, they returned to the Mississippi River and sailed to the Gulf Coast. About three hundred survivors of the original expedition went to Mexico, Peru, or back to Spain.

After De Soto, other Europeans ventured into the domain of the Southern Indians. France, England, Spain, and later the United States, all claimed tribal lands. The first Americans found themselves surrounded by white people fighting for control of the Southern Indians' world.

The sacred fire and corn ritual was part of the green corn ceremony observed by the Southern tribes. Four logs have been laid in the form of a cross around a new fire which the priest (also called the medicine man or shaman) has started by twirling a fire drill in sand. Then the priest places four ears of corn in the fire, an offering of thanksgiving to the Breath Make for another year. From this sacred fire all household fires will be kindled anew.

3

The
Indian
Way

Indian ways of looking at and doing things differed radically from those of the white people who invaded their world. These differences made it hard for the two peoples to adjust to each other. Today the white world seems more willing to understand the values and beliefs of the Indian American.

Important to the Indians were the institutions of family and clan, their beliefs about the spirit world, and their feeling about the land.

Clans and Families

The basis of tribal life was the family and the clan. In prehistoric times small family units formed the bands that followed the best hunting or farmlands. Later on, people organized themselves into clans. A clan was a group of persons who traced themselves back through the female line to a common ancestor. Clan membership was the most important alliance in a Southern Indians' life.

A clan was sometimes named for an animal or totem, a term meaning "brother," indicating the Indian concept of close human and animal relationships. The totems were regarded as the clans' supernatural ancestors or spiritual guardians. For example, a member of the Bear Clan might attach a bear skin above the door of his house.

This Seminole boy was about ten years old when George Catlin painted him in 1840.

Clan membership came through the mother. Children belonged to their mother's clan, and the mother named them. Control of children was in the mother's hands. When the time came for a boy to learn manly pursuits, the responsibility fell to an uncle on the mother's side, not the father.

Women owned the houses and their furnishings. When a woman married, her husband moved in with her. If she wanted a divorce, she simply took his possessions and set them outside the house. These customs gave women an important place in Indian society. Women also enjoyed security; if orphaned or widowed they knew the tribe would look after them. This fact helps us to understand why some pioneer white women who had lived among the Indians refused the chance to return home.

The Indian woman's advantages did not mean she did not work hard. The woman cared for the children, cooked, tended the house, tanned skins, wove baskets, and cultivated the fields. The men had the responsibility of hunting and fishing and managing tribal affairs such as ceremonies, war raids, and treaties.

Certain women, known as Beloved Women, wielded great power. Such women were Nancy Ward of the Cherokees and Mary Bosomworth of the Creeks. Ward gained her place by a heroic act, and Bosomworth came by her position as niece of a powerful chief. (See pp. 92-93, 109-10).

If the family was broken up by separation or death, the children belonged to the mother's family. Adoption was common; a child was taken into a family by the simple act of being allowed to eat from the family bowl.

Children enjoyed much freedom. The boys learned how to use the blowgun and the bow and arrow, and to play ball games. Even while they were young the boys tried to prove themselves by showing how much pain they could endure, when a young man was ready to be recognized as a warrior he was required to submit to a beating without showing any sign of suffering.

Children were usually named after animals or for something special that happened at the time of their birth. Later they received new names in recognition of achievement or as an indication of a personal characteristic. Among the Choctaws, for example, the word *humma*, meaning "red," was often added to a man's name as a mark of distinction. Many war names ended in *abi*, meaning "killer. The white people heard this as "tubbee," found often in Choctaw names of the white man's era.

The Spirit World

The Southern Indians recognized a supreme being. The Creeks called him the Breath Maker, or Master of Breath. The Cherokees called him, Yowa, but his name was too sacred to be even spoken aloud. This god resided in the sky and was the source of warmth, light, and life itself. The sun was his symbol in the sky, and fire—hot like the sun—represented him on earth. In Creek towns a sacred fire, tended by priests, was kept burning constantly.

The Southern Indians also believed there were spirits everywhere, some good, some evil. Every tree, bird, animal had a spirit that must not be offended. Woe to the Indian who killed a deer and did not ask its pardon.

Medicine men—also called priests or shamans—helped to deal with the spirit world. The Indians believed that the medicine men had direct contact with the supernatural world and could placate the spirits that caused illness or misfortune. Tribal members, led by the medicine men, engaged in elaborate ceremonies and rituals designed to keep them in good relation with the spirit world.

The white men watched the singing and dancing at these ceremonies and could make no sense of them. De Soto and most Europeans after him spoke of the Indians as "heathens." French and Spanish priests of the Roman Catholic Church tried to make Christians of them, but the Indians understood the white men's religion no better than the white men understood theirs.

As time went by, Christian missionaries went among

To cure an infection, a Timucua puffs on a pipe while a female healer offers him tobacco leaves. Jacques Le Moyne made this drawing in Florida in 1564.

The sacred pipe (calumet, or peace pipe) used in ceremonies measured one foot or longer. Indians may have lain on the ground to smoke it because of its weight and length.

the Southern tribes. They converted some of the half-bloods, mainly Choctaws and Cherokees, but the full-blooded Indians held to the beliefs of their ancestors.

What the white men failed to recognize was that the Indians' life centered around everyday practices that expressed their religious beliefs.

One such belief was the Indians' feeling about tobacco. To them tobacco was a sacred plant. They believed it was a gift from the spirit world and that it had mystical powers. They used it in many different ways. They smoked to ward off evil spirits and to bring forth friendly ones. They smoked to curb appetite and cure infection. They smoked as a gesture of friendliness to strangers, and they smoked before they waged war.

Ceremonial pipes were among the most sacred possessions of a tribe. They were beautifully designed: the bowl carved from stone and decorated with animals or human figures, the stem adorned with feathers or other material. In a tribal or town meeting, a ceremonial pipe was passed around the council. Each member took a puff before handing the pipe to the person on his left. Since smoking with former enemies was the sign a peace treaty had been made, the pipe came to be referred to as a peace pipe. The French people called the pipe a calumet, a French word meaning flute or reed.

White settlers learned about tobacco from the Indians and started cultivating it for their own use. The tobacco plant that the Indians and white settlers cultivated was smaller and more compact than the plant grown today.

Another belief related to the spirit world concerned the black drink. The Southern Indians believed this strong dark brew was a gift from the Master of Breath. The drinking of it accompanied many ceremonies. It was used before a war raid, before a stickball game, at an important council meeting, and as part of the green corn celebration (see pp. 85-87). When a young man reached maturity, he was allowed to taste it for the first time as part of his puberty rites.

The black drink was brewed like a tea from the leaves of a holly plant

Timucuas drink and vomit the black drink at a council meeting. Women heat the brew which is being passed in a large conch shell.

(*ilex vomitoria*). It contained caffeine. When heated and drunk in large quantities, it caused vomiting. The Indians believed that by emptying their stomachs in this way they rid themselves of evil. They became purified in both body and soul, ready to take part in religious ceremonies.

A Sacred Trust

One belief that whites found especially hard to understand was how the Indians felt about land.

The land itself was sacred, the center of the universe for each tribe or clan. It could not be bought or sold. Tecumseh said he could no more sell the land than he could sell the air or the sea.

Land-hungry settlers looked at Indian land, fertile and inviting. To them it appeared wasted because it was not fully cultivated. "Sell off Indian land" became the slogan as whites rushed to claim "public lands." Before the race was over, the tribes had not only lost their homeland but had been removed to Oklahoma.

Today we see what has happened to our land as we have cast aside the lessons of Indian ecology. We have not lived in harmony with the natural world as the Indians did. We have upset the balance in nature as we have exploited our natural world, our rivers, our seas. We see now the wisdom of the Indian way.

"In desperate struggles for the ball, hundreds of strong young Indian athletes were running together and leaping, actually over each other's head, and darting between their adversaries' legs, tripping and throwing, and foiling each other in every possible manner, and every voice raised to its highest key in shrill yelps and barks." This is how George Catlin, 19th-century artist, described the Choctaw ball game he also painted on canvas. The illustration is a detail of the one on page 55.

4

Choctaws, Master Farmers and Ball Players

A legend says that the Choctaws came from far in the west, guided by a sacred pole that was carried by their leader. Every night he thrust the pole into the ground where the people camped. Each morning they awoke to find the pole leaning to the east, a signal to continue the journey. When they reached Nanih Waiya [na-nee WAY-uh] the pole stood upright, and they knew this spot was to be their home.

Today a great mound called Nanih Waiya still stands near Noxapater, Mississippi, in the heart of Choctaw country. Another legend says that the Choctaws' ancestors came out of a hole or cave under a mound and moved out to occupy the surrounding region.

Whatever legend says, it is probably true that the Choctaws and the Chickasaws came as one people into the South, spreading themselves from the Tennessee River to central Florida. Later the two groups separated, the Choctaws living in what is now southwest Alabama and central and south Mississippi, and the Chickasaws living to the north.

A friendly and peaceable people, the Choctaws were excellent farmers. They were traders, too. The Choctaw language was the basis for a trade language used all across the South between Indians speaking several languages and white people speaking several European languages. This trade language was called the Mobilian trade jargon.

The Choctaws loved ball games, feasting, and dancing but were not as interested in religious ceremonies as some of the other tribes of the South.

They were small people, growing to about 5 feet 6 inches as adults. In contrast, the Natchez, the Choctaws' neighbors to the west, were often six feet tall. The Choctaws' cousins, the Chickasaws, were also taller.

The name *Choctaw* was first used for this tribe sometime around the year 1700. Choctaw is the English form of the Indian word *chahta*. It may mean "red," or it may have come from a French word meaning "flat." Some Choctaws flattened the heads of their babies.

Farmers

The Choctaws spent much of their time farming. They grew corn, beans, squash, melons, pumpkins, usually in plots beside their houses.

They cleared the land by burning the underbrush and killing the trees by tearing off the bark. They broke up the soil with hoes made of bent sticks or bison shoulder blades or pieces of flint. They practiced such good farming methods that they grew more corn and beans than they needed for themselves and were able to sell the surplus to their neighbors, the Chickasaws.

Choctaws and other Southern Indians used corn in many different ways. It was roasted or boiled while green, parched and pounded into meal when dry. Indians ate mush, dumplings, hominy, succotash—all made from corn. They made moccasins, masks, and dolls from dried cornhusks. Corncob fires, almost smokeless, heated their houses.

Each family stored its supply of corn in a crib built on poles about eight feet off the ground. To grind the corn into flour, the women put it in a rounded-out container made by burning a hollow in the side of a fallen tree, and mashed it with a wooden club-shaped instrument.

The Choctaws gathered nuts, fruits, seeds, and roots from the woods and stored them. Hunting took second place to

Using a hoe made of an animal's shoulder blade tied to a wooden handle, a woman cultivates a corn and bean patch. Hoes were also made of stone or shell.

When the corn ripened, birds had to be frightened away from eating it before it could be gathered. A woman standing on a platform waves a piece of cloth to scare the birds.

After the corn was picked and dried, it was also the woman's job to pound the corn into meal. Here she uses a weighted stick, but sometimes the pounding was done with a stone.

A young Choctaw of Mississippi carries on a tribal tradition as he shucks an ear of corn.

farming, but the men showed skill in stalking and killing game: deer, bears, and many smaller animals such as turkeys, raccoons, rabbits, pigeons, beavers, squirrels, opossums. The men used bows and arrows, while boys killed birds and small animals with blowguns made of cane and loaded with small arrows.

Fishing was sometimes done with spears and arrows, but more often by dragging ponds with nets made of brush fastened together with vines. Sometimes fish were caught after they were drugged with berries.

The Choctaws never wasted fish or animals. If they caught any extra, they divided their surplus with neighboring towns.

After coming into contact with the white people, the Choctaws learned how to use metal tools in farming. To their crops they added cotton; they had spinning wheels and spun and wove cotton cloth. They also raised chickens and cattle and pigs.

Since they were farmers, the Choctaws built their houses some distance from each other. One of their first white visitors noted that a dwelling might be as far from the next house as you could shoot a gun. Even though spaced out, a group of farmhouses made a town or settlement. In the 1700s, reports by the English, French, and Spanish listed a total of 115 Choctaw villages.

The only fortified Choctaw towns were on their tribal borders. Between neighboring tribes land was sometimes set apart as neutral ground, and it was often used by both tribes for hunting. Pickens County in Alabama, for example, was a neutral area between the Creeks and the Choctaws.

Stickball Players

But all was not work for the Choctaws. They loved to play ball. Their favorite game, stickball, was one which the other tribes also played (the northern version was called lacrosse), but it seems the Choctaws entered into it more enthusiastically than the others. It was so important that it is

Wielding their webbed sticks, stickball players (below) fight to gain control of the ball. Violence rules in a bloody struggle that included tackling, hitting, stomping. The game was well named Little Brother of War. In another Catlin painting (right), Tul-lock-chish-ko, an outstanding Choctaw ball player, wears the official costume of the game: tail made of white horsehair and a mane around his neck made of horsehair dyed various colors.

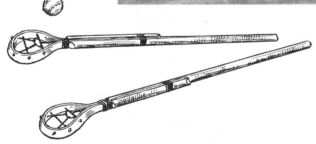

Choctaws in Mississippi today play stickball with as much spirit as their ancestors. The referee (in dark glasses) hurries to get out of the melee.

often called simply "the ball game." Whole towns took part.

Stickball was played as part of the green corn ceremony. (See p. 85.) Also called the Little Brother of War, the game served as a way to let off steam, to ease tension and to settle arguments between groups and towns. It could be so rough that players broke arms and legs, or occasionally were killed.

Each team had sixty or more players. Each player used two sticks or rackets. The racket, about 27 inches long, had a cup-like hoop at one end in which the hard deerskin ball, about the size of a golf ball, could be caught in flight. The players could not touch the ball, but caught it in the racket and threw it with the racket.

The game started with both teams lined up facing each other. The field was sometimes longer than a football field. A medicine man threw the ball high in the center of the field. An instant struggle began on the crowded field as the players tried to get the ball between the goals for a score. There were shrill cries, tripping, wrestling, and fistfights. Sometimes the ball was lost in the mass of players fighting to pick it up with their sticks. The only restriction was against using the racket on another player.

Sometimes the game, which had started in the morning,

went on to sunset. But usually after an hour or two both sides had had enough.

Since stickball was an important part of the green corn ceremony, much ritual surrounded it. First the players received a bath, drank the black drink, and danced all night.

Before play started, women from both sides came onto the field between the two teams, dancing and chanting, calling on the spirit powers to give their team victory. Much betting accompanied the game; the women placed the bets, which included everything from personal clothing and household goods to horses and weapons.

Choctaws still play stickball in the six Mississippi counties where they lived today. (See p. 151.)

Chunkey was another favorite game of the Choctaws. Like stickball, it was played by other Southern Indians. (See p.86.)

Strange Customs

The Choctaws had some unusual customs. One of these was head flattening, a habit picked up from Siouan [SOO-un] people who were absorbed by the Choctaws when they first moved into the South. We do not know exactly why the Choctaws flattened the heads of their children; they may have thought that flat heads were handsome. Or, a flat head may have been a symbol of status.

One method of head flattening was to place the baby on a flat cradle board that was hinged so that it pressed the skull. In another method, the baby's head was pressed against the board with leather strips attached to sandbag weights.

A Choctaw baby lies on a craddleboard equipped with a hinge that, when tightly bound, applied pressure to the skull and changed the shape of the head.

Another distinctive custom, also picked up from the Siouans, was long hair. In fact, the first written record of the Choctaws tells that the Spanish explorer De Soto in 1540 entered a province called Psafalaya [suh-fuh-LYE-uh]. This name means "long hair."

The most unusual custom of the Choctaws was the way they buried the dead. The body of a dead person was covered with skins and bark and placed on a raised platform near the house. Food, drink, clothing, favorite utensils and ornaments—all to help the dead person on his journey to the other world—were placed near the body. To provide companionship for the journey, a dog was killed and placed with the body. A fire was built close by and kept burning to provide warmth and light for the journey.

The body stayed on the platform for several months, to give it time to decompose. During this time family and friends came regularly to cry over the loss of the loved one.

At the end of the period, bone pickers or "buzzard men," highly respected people in the community, came to pick whatever flesh was left from the bones. When the bones were clean, they were put in a basket or box and taken to the town's bone house. At special times all the boxes of bones were taken out of the bone house and brought to a central place in the village where mourning ceremonies were held. Then the boxes were buried in a mound of earth.

Government

The Choctaw tribe was divided into three districts, each with a chief. Each chief had one or more assistants known as second chiefs or subchiefs.

Every town also had a chief, who was under the authority of the district chief. In addition, a war chief led the men of the village when the tribe went to war. Men who had distinguished themselves in fighting or in another way were known as Beloved Men.

The district chief—and the three district chiefs acting together for the whole tribe—could call a council meeting to discuss matters of peace or war or relations with the white man. Runners were sent to tell all the town chiefs about the meeting. They carried bundles of sticks, each of which was given to a chief with the instruction that a stick was to be discarded each day, and the meeting was to take place on the day when all the sticks were gone.

Council meetings were orderly and dignified, but Choctaw orators often spoke with fiery eloquence. Although ordinary people did not participate in the council discussions, they came to listen to the speeches and to join in the feasting and games and dancing that followed the councils.

The Choctaws and the Whites

As he traveled through the South from 1539 to 1542, De Soto often treated the Indians cruelly. After encountering several other tribes, he met the people who would later be called the Choctaws. in 1540 these people fought back against the white invaders. In a blood battle at Maubila (north of today's Mobile, Alabama—probably in Clarke County) Indian warriors fought furiously before being overwhelmed by the men wearing metal armor and riding horseback. (See p. 39.)

After De Soto's visit, it was 150 years before the Choctaws were bothered by the white people again. By the year 1700 traders had begun bringing European goods to Choctaw towns. The French, who had moved into the lower Mississippi Valley, became close neighbors. Now the Choctaws found their intertribal trade routes were becoming connecting links between the rival groups of white men.

Each of the European groups tried to persuade the Choctaws to help them in their struggles to gain control of valuable trade and lands. The white men did not hesitate to stir up bad feelings between the Choctaws and their Indian neighbors, the Natchez and the Chickasaws.

For a long time the Choctaws were friendly with the French. The French had established a fur-trading empire in Canada and needed the help of the Choctaws who lived where the river boats ended their journey from the north.

A Frenchman named Bienville, who had founded Mobile, built Fort Tombecbe in Choctaw country in 1735. Located near present-day Epes, Alabama, on the Tombigbee River, the fort served as a base from which the French and their Choctaw allies could hold back the British and their Chickasaw allies. It was also a trading post where furs and French goods changed hands. In 1763, when the French were forced out of America, the British moved into the fort and renamed it Fort York. But the British never succeeded in winning the Choctaws' friendship and abandoned the fort.

Now, briefly, the Spanish entered the scene. They feared that the young United States would try to expand to the southwest, so they persuaded the Choctaws to sell them a tract of land on the Tombigbee River. In 1780 the Spanish rebuilt the fort, calling it Fort Confederation.

During the American Revolution, Choctaw warriors served under Generals Washington, Morgan, Wayne, and Sullivan. Later, in the Creek Indian War (1813-14), the Choctaws fought on the side of the United States.

After the Revolution, the new American republic realized it would be to its advantage to stay friendly with the Choctaws. The US invited Choctaw chiefs in 1786 to come to Hopewell, South Carolina, where the first treaty between the Choctaw Nation and the United States was signed. The treaty set the boundaries of Choctaw hunting lands, promised US protection, and arranged for trading posts.

How the Choctaws Lost Their Land

But it became harder and harder for the United States to hold to its friendly policy with the Indians. White settlers, hungry for new land, kept moving southwestward even though the US had promised to protect Indian lands. The whites pressed for the right to what they felt was open land.

Although some in the Government wanted to be fair to the Indians, they found themselves saying: "The settlers will develop the land and make it productive, which the Indians have not done (this was not fully true). We must urge the Indians to move out of harm's way. If they were further away, in the unclaimed and undesirable western territory, they would be in less danger from whites."

That is why many treaties were signed between the United States and the Choctaws, each one calling for the Choctaws to yield more of their land.

In 1816 George Gaines, a US agent for Indian affairs, built a trading post about a hundred yards from where Fort Tombecbe once stood. At this post in that same year the three district chiefs, Pushmataha, Moshulatubbee, and Puckshenubbee, met with a US delegation and signed a treaty giving up all their tribal land east of the Tombigbee River. The agreement made it legal for hundreds of white settlers to enter the region.

In 1820 at Doak's Stand (Mississippi) the same three Choctaw chiefs agreed to move to the west. But their hearts were not in it. Pushmataha pointed out to General Andrew Jackson, who represented the United States, that his people were giving up rich lands in exchange for an area that was already partly settled (Oklahoma and Arkansas). When the Choctaws refused to leave, Mississippi passed state laws abolishing the tribal government and took other measures to frighten the Indians into leaving.

The Indian Removal Act of 1830, passed by the US Congress, gave President Jackson the power to send to the west the tribes that lived east of the Mississippi. In September of that year, at Dancing Rabbit Creek, Mississippi, the Choctaws signed away the last bit of their ancient homeland.

The Choctaws were the first of the five Southern tribes to move as a nation to the Indian Territory. The people traveled mostly on foot, in groups of 500 to 1,000. Each fall for three years (1831-33), groups left Mississippi on the 400-mile trip. US agents and army officers supervised the journeys. Hundreds of people died on the way, victims of the winter blizzards, epidemics of cholera and other diseases, lack of supplies, and accidents.

Not all the Choctaws left Mississippi. The Treaty of

The Choctaw Nation at the time the tribe first made contact with the Europeans.

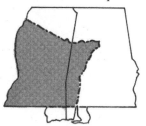

After 1765 cession to British.

After 1801 Ft. Adams Treaty.

After 1802 treaty.

Dancing Rabbit Creek had allowed a few to stay on their lands. Several thousand more simply refused to leave. In 1843 a Choctaw known only as Cobb tried to explain to a US agent how his people felt:

"Brother: When you were young we were strong. We fought by your side. But our arms are now broken. You have grown large; my people have become small.

"Brother: My voice is weak. It is not the shout of a warrior but the wail of an infant. I have lost it in mourning over the misfortunes of my people. These are their graves; and in those aged pines you hear the ghosts of the departed. Their ashes are here, and we have been left to protect them. Our warriors are nearly all gone to the far country west. But here are our dead. Shall we go, too, and give their bones to the wolves?

"Brother: When you took our country, you promised us land. There is your promise in the book. Twelve times have the trees dropped their leaves, and yet we have received no land. Our houses have been taken from us. The white man's plow turns up the bones of our fathers. We dare not kindle our fires; and yet you said we might remain and you would give us land."

Today about 5,000 Choctaws live in east central Mississippi, in the neighborhood of Philadelphia. Over 90 percent of these people still speak their native language.

A Nation Shrinks and Disappears:

How the Choctaws their lands, bit by bit, to the whites

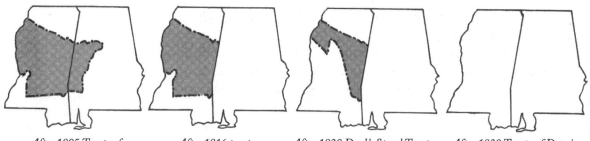

After 1805 Treaty of Mt. Dexter

After 1816 treaty

After 1820 Doak's Stand Treaty

After 1830 Treaty of Dancing Rabbit Creek

Famous Choctaws

PUSHMATAHA: The best known of all Choctaw chiefs was Pushmataha. He was born in 1764 in Noxubee County, Mississippi. As a young man he became a leader in the tribe by proving himself in war, hunting, and ball playing. He once led a hunting party chasing buffalo across the Mississippi River into the Red River area of Louisiana. Hostile Indians attacked his group, but Pushmataha escaped to a Spanish settlement where he lived for five years, supporting himself by hunting. After he returned home, he headed a war party and, as was the Choctaw custom, revenged himself on the Indians who had attacked him earlier.

This portrait of the great Choctaw chief Pushmataha by Charles Bird King appears in The McKenney-Hall Portrait Gallery of American Indians.

Pushmataha had been only a boy during the American Revolution, when his people sided with the colonists. After the war the Choctaws promised the US their "perpetual peace and friendship." When he became chief of the Southern Choctaw District, Pushmataha cooperated with the United States. He traveled to Mobile to offer his services in punishing the Creeks who had attacked white settlers at Fort Mims. Five thousand Choctaw warriors, assembled at the national council grounds, debated whether to support the chief in this action. Pushmataha argued that their friends were not the Creeks but the people at St. Stephens (near Fort Mims) with whom they had played ball. Drawing out his sword, he said: "You can all do as you please. You are all free men. I dictate to none of you. But I shall join the St. Stephens people. If you have a mind to follow me, I will lead you to glory and victory." A shout went up from the warriors, each man saying, "I will follow you." The Pushmataha Battalion was formed, and Pushmataha led the Choctaw warriors against the British and their allies from other Indian tribes. He kept open supply routes through the South that were vital to the US and was given the honorary title of general.

Pushmataha wanted the Choctaws to get along with their white neighbors and please the US agents living among them. He urged his people to attend schools, learn more about farming, and shop at the trading posts. Despite these efforts to please the whites, the US persisted in its plan to take the rich Choctaw lands and move the Indians to Arkansas. Pushmataha opposed the removal. He knew the land from his youthful hunting days. "I have often had my feet severely bruised by the roughness of its surface," he said.

In 1820 authorities discovered that white settlers already occupied the area designated in the Doak's Stand Treaty. In 1824 a delegation of Choctaws journeyed to Washington to discuss the problem. Pushmataha addressed the Secretary of War:

"Father, you have no doubt heard of me; I am Pushmataha. When in my own country, I often looked toward this Council House, and wanted to come here. I am in trouble. I feel like a small child not half as high as its father. So, Father, I hang in the bend of your arm, and look in your face.

"When I was in my own country, I heard there were men appointed to talk to us. I would not speak there; I chose to come here, and speak in this beloved house.

"I can boast and say, and tell the truth, that none of my fathers, or grandfathers, nor any Choctaw ever drew bows against the United States. They have always been friendly. We have held the hands of the United States so long that our nails are long like bird's claws; and there is no danger of their slipping out.

"I came here when a young man to see my Father Jefferson. He told me if ever we got in trouble we must run and tell him. I am come."

While he was in Washington, Pushmataha, now sixty years old, fell ill. He called his companions to him, asking them to bring his guns and put his decorations on him.

"Let the big guns be fired over me," he said. "I shall die, but you will return to our brethren. When you shall come to your home, they will as you, 'Where is Pushmataha?' and you will say to them, 'He is no more.' They will hear the tidings like the sound of the fall of a mighty oak in the stillness of the woods."

The famous chief died December 24, 1824, and was buried

in the Congressional National Cemetery in Washington, with full honors. Guns were fired from Capitol Hill, and a mile-long procession with troops of cavalry and a band escorted Pushmataha to his final resting place. John Randolph of Virginia gave a funeral oration in the US Senate, and President James Monroe sent a presidential medal to Pushmataha's oldest son.

GREENWOOD LEFLORE: Greenwood LeFlore was born in 1800 at LeFleur's Bluff (now Jackson, Mississippi) and named for an English sea captain. His father was an adventurous French Canadian who ran a trading post on the Natchez Trace. His mother was Rebecca Crevat, a niece of Pushmataha; that kinship assured LeFlore of an honored place among the Choctaws.

Major John Donlevy, who owned a stage line on the Trace, became interested in young LeFlore and sent him to Nashville to be educated. In 1819 LeFlore married Donlevy's daughter Rose and returned to Mississippi to live.

In 1824 the Choctaw Nation for the first time chose its head chief by general election. The honor went to the young and handsome LeFlore. Chief LeFlore worked hard to get schools for the Choctaws and to train them to live in the white man's world. But when he agreed to the sale of Choctaw lands, he was called a traitor by his tribe.

Moshulatubbee, a district chief of the Choctaws in Mississippi, moved with his people to Oklahoma. Catlin made this portrait in 1834 after the removal.

It was due to LeFlore's influence, however, that the US agreed that any Choctaw who wished could remain in Mississippi and receive a section of land. LeFlore chose to stay; but he found himself rejected by his tribe, even by the group of Choctaws who remained. He turned to the white people's world, and between 1840 and 1860 he became a wealthy cotton planter. He served in the state legislature in both the House and the Senate.

Near Greenwood, on the spot where LeFlore had lived in a log cabin, he built a white-columned mansion called Malmaison. Furnishings were designed for him in Paris, and scenic wallpaper from France and Switzerland hung on the walls. In the library, under a portrait of LeFlore, hung a sword and belt presented to him by the US Government upon his election as chief.

When the War Between the States started, LeFlore refused to give up his US citizenship to join the Confederacy. He found himself rejected by both the Southern whites and the Choctaws. All during the war the US flag flew over Malmaison. When LeFlore died in 1865 his body was wrapped in the flag of the United States. He was buried on a hillside near Malmaison.

Malmaison burned in the 1940s, but reminders of LeFlore live on in the names of the city of Greenwood and of LeFlore County and in his descendants who live today in Mississippi.

Sounds and Meanings

Choctaw Place Names Used Today

Name and location	How to pronounce	What it means
Alamuchee Creek, Ala.	ah-lah-MOO-chee	Hiding places are there.
Coatopa, Ala.	koe-ah-TOE-pah	Creek where the panther is hurt.
Conehatta, Ala.	koe-neh-HAH-tah	White skunk—probably because an albino skunk was seen here.
Cushtusha Creek, Miss.	kush-tush-ah	("kush" and "tush" as in "push") Fleas are there.
Hopoca, Miss.	hoe-POE-kah	Final gathering place.
Itta Bena, Miss.	IT-tah BEE-nah	Home in the woods.
Mobile, Ala.	moe-BEEL	To paddle.
Panola, Miss.	puh-NOE-luh	Cotton.
Pascagoula, Miss.	pass-kah-GOO-lah	Singing river. Legend says the mourning sound heard on the river is connected to the death of the Pascagoula tribe, who walked into the river and drowned rather than face subjection by the Biloxi tribe.
Pelahatchie, Miss.	peh-lah-HATCH-ee	Hurricane stream.
Puss Cuss, Ala.		Crying child creek.
Shuqualak, Miss.	SHOOK-wah-lack	Hog wallow.
Tibbie, Miss.		Water fighting. This stream formed a part of the Choctaw-Chickasaw boundary where the two tribes fought each other.
Timmillichee's Ford, Ala.	tih-mih-LEECH-ee	He who strikes once with the hell of the hand. Named for a chief who lived in a settlement near by.
Tombigbee River, Ala.		Box- or coffin-makers. Old men whose job it was to clean the bones of the dead and place them in boxes evidently lived along this river.
Toomsuba, Miss.	toom-SOO-bah	Pigeon hawk or blue darter; or, deer hunters' town.
Yalobusha, Miss.	yah-loe-BOO-shah	Little tadpole.
Yazoo, Miss.	YAH-zoo	River of death. Site of a battle between two tribes.

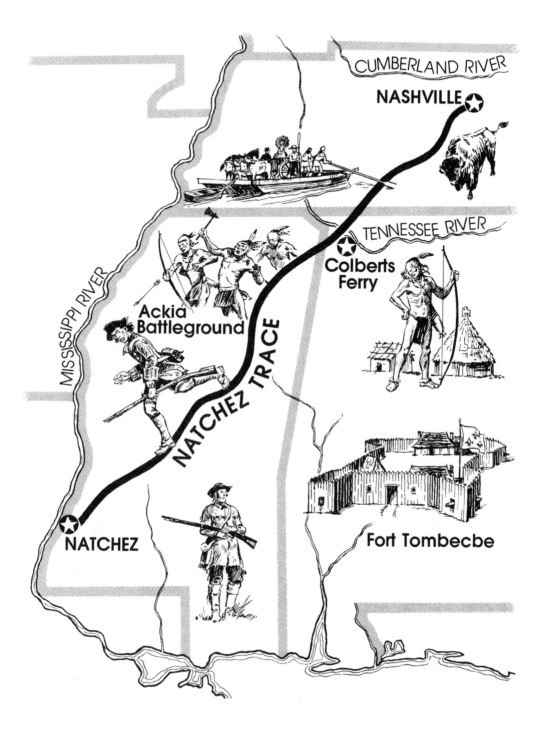

The Natchez Trace ran through the heart of Chickasaw country. Many roads, like the Trace, began as buffalo trails, then became Indian paths, then pioneer roads, and finally the highways we travel today. Colbert's Ferry was a favorite overnight stop on the Trace. The Chickasaw chief George Colbert operated the ferry and also offered lodging, for a fee, in his house.

5

Chickasaws, Skilled Warriors

Famed for their military skill, the Chickasaws were masters of the ambush and the surprise attack. It was said they could chase a fleeing enemy at a "long gallop."

Although smaller in number than the other Southern tribes (never more than 5,000), they claimed a large region and are remembered for their courageous defense of their territory. Their land ranged from northeast Mississippi into northwest Alabama and north into Tennessee and Kentucky and even Ohio.

Without the Chickasaws, North American history might have been very different. When the British and the French were struggling for control of the Mississippi River and the trade it made possible, the Chickasaws sided with the British. Repeatedly and successfully they attacked the French. If the Chickasaws had liked the French instead of the British, the nation of France might have been the one to settle the new nation—and most Southerners today might be speaking French.

The Art of Warfare

Long before they met the white people, however, the Chickasaws had a different feeling about warfare. Like the other Southern Indians, the Chickasaws early in their tribal history had little desire to conquer or do away with another tribe or acquire another tribe's land or possessions. Warfare was more show than actual strife. It was conducted with much ceremony and with less killing than war in Europe at the same time.

Swift raids by small war parties were the usual pattern of warfare by the Southern Indians. Such raids occurred in retaliation for raids made on the attackers. So there never was an end to raiding back and forth. This situation was exactly what the Indians wanted, since the raids gave the young men a chance to prove their bravery and become warriors and the older men opportunity to practice their war-making skills.

The success of a raid depended on how well the prewar ceremonies were observed. Each town had a war chief or Great Warrior who supervised the three-day preparation for the raid. The men ate nothing, but drank the black drink, which caused them to vomit. This purified them for battle. To spur the young men on, the older men told about brave deeds they had done. They painted their bodies with war paint and danced while they sang death songs.

Thirty or forty men might make up a raiding party. They left the town with a great display of courage, chanting war songs as they went. Once in the woods, however, they moved quietly on moccasined feet. Each man carried a bow and arrows, a knife and a war club stuck through his belt. The war club, spiked with fish teeth, was used in hand-to-hand fighting. A man's back pack held a blanket, a bag of parched cornmeal, a wooden cup, and leather to repair his moccasins. The warrior may have carried a shield of woven cane to protect himself.

The object of a raid was to surprise the enemy. To do this the raiding party split up into groups of three or four, each group traveling single file. They stepped in each other's tracks to make it appear the footsteps were made by a single person. They kept in touch with each other by imitating animal sounds. For instance, a war party would send out scouts in four directions. The scout to the right imitated the call of an owl if he saw the enemy; the scout at the left, a wolf; the one in the rear, a fox; and the one in front, a bird. The Chickasaws were expert trackers. They could pick up telltale signs left by other Indians and determine what tribe and town they belonged to.

A Chickasaw war party prepares for a raid.

If the war party succeeded in surprising the enemy, the attackers might be satisfied with just touching their victims with special sticks. This touching was considered as brave an act as killing since it required considerable skill. At other times the war party might take a few scalps. (Indians did little scalping before the white man came. A scalping knife was part of every pioneer's equipment and was freely used on Indians. In fact, the colonial European governments often offered bounties for Indian scalps.)

When a successful war party returned home, the town celebrated for three days with singing, dancing, and feasting. Part of the celebration centered around the young men who had proved their bravery. They were given war names. They had earned the right to wear a certain feather in their headdress and to tattoo records of their deeds on their bodies. No longer did they have to tend fires, light pipes, and serve the older men. They were warriors.

Sometime after they met the white man, who brought the horse to the New World, the Chickasaws developed a special breed of ponies, fast and sturdy, that helped them maintain their reputation as fighters. Every year they made raids west of the Mississippi River to bring back bars of silver and copper, which they made into ornaments.

Sometimes the Indians tired of this raiding back and forth. They settled for a game of stickball, called the Little Brother of War. (See p. 54.)

Cousins to the Choctaws

The name of the Chickasaws shows that they were closely related to the Choctaws. It means, in the Choctaw language, "They left as a tribe not a very great while ago." The two tribes separated sometime before the arrival of the white man, and were often hostile to each other. But they shared the same language and many of the same customs.

Many Chickasaw towns were built along the Tombigbee and Yazoo Rivers in Mississippi. One of their main settlements was at Chickasaw Old Fields, a beautiful plain near

Tupelo, Mississippi. The first Chickasaw Old Fields, however, was located in Alabama on the Tennessee River east of Muscle Shoals. The Chickasaws left that location and went west to Mississippi when Cherokees moved in from the east. Pontotoc was the capital of the Chickasaws in the 1700s.

The Chickasaws were taller than their Choctaw cousins, the men usually between five feet ten inches and six feet tall. They had light reddish skin and dark hair and eyes. They carried themselves with dignity and took great pride in their reputation as successful traders and skilled fighters.

In winter they slept in cabins in which a chimney-less fire burned all night; in the morning they jumped into pools of cold water. This hot-house-and-cold-bath treatment was also used to cure the sick.

The Chickasaws did little farming. They bought much of their food from the neighboring Choctaws. Whatever farming was done was done by women. Hunting small game for food was left to the boys.

In their tribal government, the Chickasaws were ruled by a chief, called *mingo* or *micco* (translated "king" by the

A Chickasaw hunter, disguised with a deerskin, stalks a deer. Deerskin, softened like velvet, made breeches, shirts, skirts, moccasins. Bones from deer made fishing hooks, farming implements, tools.

British). The chief was selected from the highest ranking clan in the tribe and served for life. Next to him was the war chief. Each clan was ruled by a subchief who came to be chief through his mother's position. This clan-inherited type of government contrasted with that of the Choctaws who selected their chiefs by merit rather than by family ties.

The Chickasaws and the Whites

The Spanish explorer De Soto entered the land of the "Chicaca" in late 1540. The first Chickasaw town he came to was on the bank of a river, possibly the Black Warrior (west Alabama). The Indians tried to protect their town, but De Soto forced them back into the river. He moved on to Mississippi and camped near the main towns of the Chickasaws. At first the Indians greeted the Spaniards with gifts, Chief Miculasa himself bringing the deerskins. But when De Soto demanded two hundred men to go with him as burden-bearers, Chickasaw warriors skillfully attacked the Spanish army at night, causing heavy losses of supplies and horses. These successful attacks helped make the Chickasaws' reputation as fighters.

We know little about the Chickasaws during the 150 years after De Soto's visit. Then, in 1698, the Chickasaws first met the British, who wanted to set up trading posts in their area. From that time to the time of the American Revolution the Chickasaws were loyal friends of the British. They greeted French traders who sailed up the Mississippi River into Chickasaw territory with well-aimed arrows from the banks. Many of the French boats did not get through to the north.

In five wars between 1736 and 1753, the Chickasaws soundly beat the French. The Chickasaws built long one-street towns, which were really strings of connecting villages. These towns, protected by picket walls, stood as effective

Bernard Romans, Dutch botanist, surveyor, and artist, who traveled among the Southern tribes in the 1750's, made this portrait of a Chickasaw.

barriers against the French on the Gulf Coast who were trying to unite with the French of Ohio against the British settlers. At the Battle of Ackia (near Tupelo, Mississippi) the Chickasaws defeated the French general Bienville, a defeat that opened the entire area to the British.

Although the American Revolution swung the Chickasaws around to the side of the new colonies (some Chickasaws served in the Revolutionary Army), from that time on the proud Indian nation gradually found itself giving up its land to the whites. In the first treaty between the Chickasaws and the United States, Chief Piomingo (George Colbert) gave up five square miles on the Tennessee River—near present-day Muscle Shoals, Alabama—for a trading post. This was in 1786.

Fifteen years later the tribe gave the US the right of way on their ancient trading path, now called the Natchez Trace. A few years after that, the Chickasaw Old Fields in Alabama was lost. In 1818 Chickasaw chiefs met with Andrew Jackson at Treaty Ground of Old Town and agreed to give up lands in Kentucky and Tennessee and sold a tract in Alabama belonging to the Colbert family.

For a few years the Chickasaws resisted pressure from the United States to yield more of their territory. But in 1832 they gave in, and in the Treaty of Pontotoc sold the last of their homelands.

Having lost their land to eager white settlers who were pouring into Tennessee, Alabama, and Mississippi, the Chickasaws began to prepare to move to a strange area, the Oklahoma Territory. Although they were the wealthiest of the Southern tribes, they suffered greatly on the long trek made in the winter of 1836-37. The last Chickasaw war chief, Tishomingo, died at age 102 on the journey and was buried near Little Rock, Arkansas. The queen of the Chickasaws, the old and revered Pakanli, also died on the journey.

In Oklahoma the Chickasaws became one of the Five Civilized Tribes who had moved from the South.

Famous Chickasaws

THE COLBERT BROTHERS: He was tall, slender, and handsome, with long straight black hair—a courageous fighter, who, it was said, once personally fought Andrew Jackson. He was hospitable to the many people who visited his home and crossed the river on his ferry. He was George Colbert, the most famous of the five Colbert brothers. The Colberts' Indian name was Piomingo.

The Colberts' father, James Logan Colbert, was a Scot who moved west from the Carolinas about 1740 and stopped at Muscle Shoals. He married a Chickasaw woman, and their son George was born about 1764.

Always friends of the United States, George and his brother William fought with General St. Clair against the northern Indians in 1792. Later three of the Colbert brothers led a war party against Cherokees, who were trying to push down to the Tennessee River. President George Washington called the brothers to the US capital in July 1794 to thank them for their service to the United States; he gave them presents, including suits of clothes, plows, and axes.

Near the spot where the Natchez Trace would cross the Tennessee River, George Colbert built a home and plantation. He also operated a ferry and a lodging and eating house for travelers at Buzzard Roost. With another plantation at Tupelo (Mississippi) and 140 slaves in all, he soon became the wealthiest man in the Chickasaw Nation.

For twelve years George Colbert was head chief of the Chickasaws. His name appears on all the important treaties between his tribe and the US. Later he gave up his place as head chief to his brother Levi, "who was greatly beloved and whose management of the nation evinced better statesmanship than that of any other chief except George Colbert." The names of William and Levi are also found on treaties.

William Colbert helped the US Army when it was sent to take over Spanish posts in the Southwest in 1798. He also fought with Andrew Jackson against the Creeks. Three of the Colbert brothers led 350 Chickasaw warriors to join

General Jackson in the Battle of New Orleans in 1815.

A white man who recognized the Indians' right to their lands and sympathized with them was Thomas L. McKenney, who served as the US Government's superintendent of Indian affairs. In the 1820s when it seemed no longer possible to keep the white settlers from moving onto Indian lands, McKenney traveled through the South to talk with tribal leaders about moving west. He met with Chickasaw chiefs at the home of Levi Colbert, at that time head of the tribe. First McKenney showed the chiefs a map of the proposed Chickasaw lands in the west. Then he lighted a peace pipe, showing the Indians that he respected their way of talking in a council meeting. In reply to McKenney's proposal, the chiefs said: "Here lie the bones of our fathers. This is the home of our infancy and we love our country. We cannot give it up."

But McKenney persuaded them to leave by saying: "Your fathers are not here. What remains of them is dust. They feel not, nor care where the foot of the white man or the red man treads on their graves. But your children live and they must be clothed and fed. And after them will come other generations of children. Forget not to provide for them."

Most of the Colbert family went west with the tribe. The dignity they showed during this humiliating experience impressed the white soldiers. Some of the Colberts dressed in their national costumes and traveled by horseback on the long journey to the new territory.

Today Colbert Country in northwest Alabama marks the old home of this remarkable Chickasaw family.

TASKI ETOKA: Taski Etoka was a high mingo (chief) of the Chickasaws, but he was very different from the Colbert brothers.

Like them, he fought for his people's independence and their right to their lands. But the way he did this was not at all like the way the Colberts went about it. Maybe the fact that he was a full-blooded Chickasaw (both his parents were Chickasaws) had something to do with this approach. Wanting to be free of the white man's influence, he did not accept European ways. For instance, he did not wear the white man's clothes.

But, although he may not have realized it, Taski Etoka's ideal of freedom from white influences was lost even before he was born. When the Chickasaws met the white traders they began giving up their old hunting ways. Now, instead of hunting for food as they had always done, they hunted for pelts to trade.

As a boy, Taski Etoka fought against the French. He was happy when finally that group of Europeans was driven from the Mississippi Valley. But although the British were supposed to be his people's friends, Taski Etoka soon found out that the white men would not allow the Chickasaws a strong voice in their own affairs. And he saw that the British could not stop the white settlers who were gradually moving into Chickasaw lands.

Taski Etoka made many long trips and spent much effort trying to persuade the white people to keep their promises and help the Chickasaws. But he died in 1794, never having succeeded in protecting his people from being overwhelmed by the white man.

Sounds and Meanings

Chickasaw Place Names Used Today

Name and location	How to pronounce	What it means
Foshee, Ala.	foe-SHEE	Bird.
Halloka Creek, Ga.	hah-LOE-kah	Beloved place.
Houlka, Miss.	HULK-uh	Sacred place. Site of tribal culture until 1832. De Soto visited here in 1541.
Killycassida Creek, Ala.	KILL-ee-kah-SEE-dah	Honey locust bent and broken.
Pontotoc, Miss.	PON-toh-tok	Battle where the cattails stood. Site of the battle (1736) in which the Chickasaws defeated the French.
Sipsey River, Ala.	SIP-see	Poplar or cottonwood tree.
Tallehoma River, Miss.	tal-eh-HOME-ah	Red rock. The river cuts through the gorge, exposing red cliffs.
Tishomingo, Miss.	tih-shoh-MING-oh	Warrior chief.
Toccopola, Miss.	toh-koe-POE-lah	The crossing of the roads.
Tuscumbia, Ala.	tuss-KUM-b'yah	Warrior killer. Named for a Cherokee chief—but his name was Chickasaw.

Creek men shave their heads, leaving a crest, or roach, from front to back. Some cropped the hair close only on one side, making it easier to draw back the arrow.

6

Creeks,
People of the
Sacred Fire

What made the Creeks different from the other Southern tribes? It was their genius for bringing many different tribes together to form a Creek nation or confederacy.

Weakened by war and the pressure from white settlers, the tribe called the Muscogees began to merge with other tribes. The alliance centered around three towns in the area now known as Georgia. By about the year 1600 the league had accepted tribes called the Alibamos, Koasatis, and Hitchitis. Later they took under their wing the Apalachees, Shawnees, Yuchis, Yamasees, Natchez, and many others. So we see that the word *tribe*, as it is used in speaking of the Cherokees or the Choctaws, does not really apply to the Creeks.

The name of a Creek tribe was often also the name of a town. Most Creek towns were located on or near riverbanks. At one time there were 55 or more Creek towns with a total population of 15,000 to 20,000 people. These people spoke half a dozen languages, observed their own customs, and had their own chiefs, but they all belonged in the Creek Confederacy. The name *Creek* was given to them by early English traders who called the Indians they found living on Ochese Creek in Georgia "Creek Indians."

The white people noted that the Creek men were of medium height, taller than their Choctaw neighbors but shorter than most Cherokees. They were well built, very strong and

Tukabatchee served as the capital of both Upper and Lower Creeks. It was here that Tecumseh made his impassioned plea for an Indian confederacy to turn back white settlers. Note the Creek Path running between the Upper Creek and Lower Creek areas. The same route is followed today between Montgomery, Alabama, and Columbus Georgia.

agile. The women tended to be short, but they too were strong. The Creeks' skin was copper red in color. The men plucked their whiskers, so their face skin was smooth.

Upper Creeks and Lower Creeks

The Creek Confederacy was divided into two groups, called by the whites the Upper Creeks and the Lower Creeks. Each division had a head chief called a *micco*. A chief had great authority. He ruled over the tribal council, sitting on a platform which raised him above the other men.

The Upper Creeks lived in about forty towns on the Coosa, Tallapoosa, and Alabama Rivers. Tallassee, Coosa, Okchai, and Okfuskee were important Upper Creek towns.

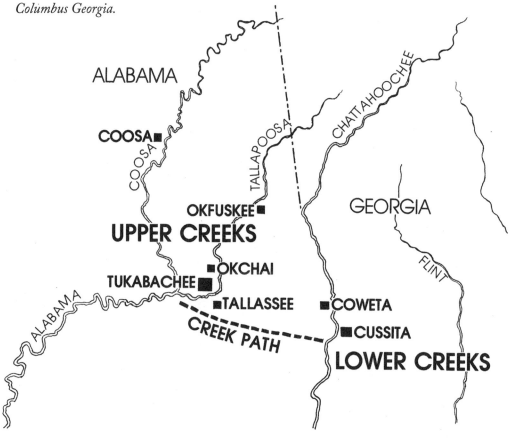

The Lower Creeks lived on the Okmulgee, Flint, and Chattahoochee Rivers in about twenty towns, of which the most important were Coweta and Cussita.

In spite of their geographical separation, the two divisions recognized a central governing body which had the final say of matters related to the confederacy as a whole.

The capital of the nation was at Tukabachee, an Upper Creek town on the Tallapoosa near present-day Montgomery, Alabama. National councils, made up of representatives from over the confederacy, met here to decide tribal matters. Both a head chief and a war chief represented the nation.

Creek Towns

Creek towns were known as either white towns or red towns. The white towns were peace towns; the people in these towns had the responsibility of carrying out ceremonies not related to war, such as the annual green corn ceremony (see pg. 85) or ball games. The principal chief of the entire nation was always chosen from a white town.

The red towns were war towns. War ceremonies were their affair. They organized war parties, led raiding expeditions, and took care of religious rituals related to war.

The Creeks lived in villages and towns, some of which had as many as a hundred houses. Family groups lived in houses spread out in all directions from the town square. A large family had a house for cooking, another to sleep in, another for storing grain. There was one kind of house for use in winter and another one for summer. Winter houses were so well insulated that the white people called them "hot houses." Summer houses were no more than rain shelters—four poles making a square, with brush for a roof. Cane mats were used for sleeping.

The Creeks made good use of animal skins in their clothing. They cured and softened such skins as deer, bear, and beaver, and fashioned them into colorful cloaks or blankets. Both men and women wore these skins thrown over their shoulders and reaching to their knees.

Council house

Square ground

A Creek village stirs with activity. In the square ground, leaders meet in the shade of an open, thatch-roofed structures. (In winter they meet in the round council house, which also is where villagers gather for ceremonies, dances, and socializing.) Two men play chunkey on the ball field. Women members of a large group bustle around the cluster of

The Creeks did not want for food. Hunters provided the townspeople with the meat of deer, bear, turkey, and buffalo. In fields outside the town many different kinds of crops were planted: corn, squash, beans, sweet potatoes. Streams and rivers running through Creek country provided fish and mussels.

Town life centered around the public square. Here stood the chief's house, the council house, and perhaps a temple mound. There might also be a house for the Beloved Men, aged and respected tribe leaders. Indians believed old people had great wisdom and the power of prophecy.

In the square or close by was the public grain storehouse to which each family in the town contributed.

Also in the square was the ball field. In this sunken area the people played their favorite games—chunkey and stickball—and held their dances and celebrations.

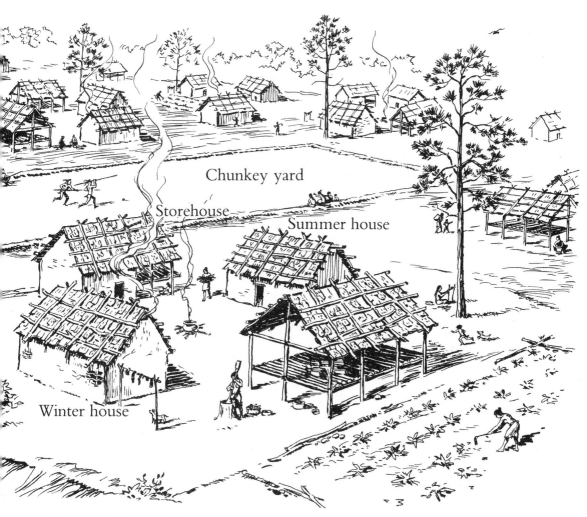

Chunkey yard

Storehouse

Summer house

Winter house

Green Corn Ceremony

The most important celebration for the Creeks, as for the other Southern tribes, was the green corn ceremony. (The white people called the ceremony the "busk," after its Creek name *poskita*, meaning "to fast.") The festival was like our Thanksgiving and New Year rolled into one. It was a time to give thanks for a successful harvest, to settle differences, and to begin a new year. The celebration took place in July or August, depending on when the corn ripened.

When the corn was about ripe, the chief of each head town sent runners to the smaller villages to tell the people when to come to the busk. The runner left a bundle of sticks in each village, with instructions to break one stick each day. When all were broken, it was time for the busk.

Unlike our Thanksgiving or New Year, the busk lasted

buildings which make up their home—an airy summer house, an enclosed winter house, and a raised storehouse for grain and other food. A vegetable garden adjoins the house.

Two persons at a time played the game of chunkey. One of the players started the game by rolling the smooth stone disk down the court. Then both players, carrying eight-foot poles flattened at the ends, raced after it. The object of the game was not to hit the stone but to throw the javelin-like pole close to the spot where the disk would stop rolling. The game took practice and skilled judgement. The player whose pole landed nearer the disk made one point; if his pole actually touched the disk, two points. The playing field for chunkey was rectangular, smoothed level with sand. Both players and spectators bet heavily on the outcome of the game.

as long as eight days. The first three days were spent cleaning and getting ready for the celebration. On the first day the men scrubbed and repaired the public buildings in the square. The women swept out the houses, even breaking up old pots.

Then the people started cleansing themselves. They fasted for two nights and a day. They took the black drink, which cleaned out their bodies and purified their minds. (See p. 48.)

On the third day the most sacred part of the busk began: the new fire ritual. All the fires in all the houses in the town were put out, even the sacred fire in the square. In each town the sacred fire was kept burning to remind the people of the presence of the Breath Maker. The Indians believed the fire was the symbol on earth of their god, the Breath Maker.

The starting of the new sacred fire was a religious rite carried out by a high priest. For the occasion he wore white buckskin clothes and white moccasins. To start the fire he used a fire drill, twirling it in sand and praying to the Breath Maker. Smoke appeared first, and then flame. Four logs, laid in the form of a cross, were

Carved and polished chunkey stones measured 5 inches across and one and one-half inches thick.

pushed toward the fire. The priest took four ears of ripe corn and placed them in the fire. In this act he made an offering of thanksgiving to the Breath Maker for another year. From this sacred fire all the household fires were started anew.

The religious part of the busk was over and the next five days were spent playing games and dancing. The women prepared food for the feast in the public square. Friendly rivalry between towns and clan was played out on the ball field. The women danced, the men danced, and then together they performed the tribal dances.

On the last day of the busk an orator respected by the tribe told the people that they must keep the ancient customs and rites in the new year. He reminded them that they were bound together because they shared the same sacred fire. People went home form the green corn ceremony feeling even more united as a tribe.

A priest starts the sacred fire.

The Creek Indian War

Because they were allied in a confederacy, the Creeks managed to hold on to their land longer than they would have as small tribes. They were first caught in the struggle of Spain, France, and Great Britain to claim the New World. Alexander McGillivray, a powerful Creek chief, proved to be a skillful diplomat. He bargained first with one country and then another, trying to save the Creek Confederacy.

During the American War for Independence the Creeks sided first with the rebelling colonists and then with the British. When the colonists won, the newly formed government of the United States declared the Creek land public land, and land-hungry whites rushed in to claim it. The Creeks held the white settlers off for a while, but after McGillivray's death in 1793 the tribe became divided. The Upper Creeks resisted the white settlers, believing the United States would protect their land rights, but the Lower Creeks saw no point in fighting the white settlers. By 1812 the once powerful Creek Confederacy, which had spread over most of Georgia and Alabama, had fallen back before the whites to a few towns along the inland rivers of Alabama.

In the Creek Indian War of 1813-14, most of the Upper Creek towns fought against Andrew Jackson and his Tennessee Volunteers. The Lower Creeks allied themselves with the whites. The warriors in all the towns voted their allegiance by throwing their sticks or tomahawks either to a white or a red side of the council fire. Those favoring war became Red Stick (Upper Creeks), the other became the White Sticks (Lower Creeks). The Creek Indian War, in fact, is sometimes called the Red Stick War.

Scattered skirmishes between the Creeks and the settlers started the Creek Indian War. A party of several hundred Creeks returning from Pensacola on a trading mission was attacked by whites at Burnt Corn Creek (in present-day Baldwin County, Alabama). Word of the attack spread among the Indians and they prepared for war. Alarmed settlers fled to Fort Mims for protection. On August 30, 1813, one thousand warriors under William Weatherford (Red

The first wave of US militia storms the Indian breastworks in the Battle of Horseshoe Bend, as shown in this diorama which can be seen at Horseshoe Bend Park. One thousand Creek warriors fell before two thousand infantry, two cannons, and six hundred Cherokees. At the Horseshoe (see the air view of what it looks like today) the once-powerful Creek Nation suffered irreparable loss.

Eagle) advanced on Fort Mims. Within a short time over 500 people in the fort were killed in one of the bloodiest massacres in American history.

"Remember Fort Mims" became the rallying cry of the settlers. For two years after that, Andrew Jackson led volunteer troops against the Creeks. He burned village after village. Weatherford meanwhile had gathered warriors around him at a place called the Holy Ground, a high bluff on the Alabama River. A medicine man had convinced the Creeks that the spot was sacred and that no white could enter it. But the medicine man was wrong. General F.L. Claiborne with his Choctaw allies stormed the Holy Ground, killing many Indians and driving the rest into the river. It was here that Weatherford made his famous jump on horseback into the Alabama River. (See p. 97.)

In March 1814, the Creeks, driven relentlessly by Jackson, prepared for a last desperate stand at Horseshoe Bend on the Tallapoosa River in Alabama. In the horseshoe-shaped bend of the river, about a thousand Creeks under the command of Chief Menawa gathered for battle. Women and children were sent down the river for safety. Canoes were hidden along the riverbank for escape. A breastwork of logs was built to protect the land approach. Jackson had at his command 2,000 foot soldiers, seven hundred cavalrymen, six hundred Cherokees, and some Lower Creeks. The Creeks fought bravely and held back the soldiers who stormed the breastwork. But they had no chance when the Cherokees and the cavalry forded the river and attacked them from the rear.

By nightfall the battle was over. Scattered over the field were over five hundred dead Creeks; another three hundred were shot trying to escape across the river. Menawa, though badly wounded, was one of the few survivors.

After the Battle of Horseshoe Bend, white settlers poured onto Creek land. William McIntosh, chief of the Lower Creeks, signed away all Creek land at the Treaty of Indian Spring in 1825. The Creek Nation was in chaos. Some of the tribal groups were ready to give up and move west to an area promised by the US, while others wanted to stay. The first Creeks moved in 1828; they were from Lower Creek towns.

A few Creek raiding parties attacked white settlements. In 1836 General Winfield Scott of the US Army, with several thousand troops and a few Lower Creek chiefs, set out to put an end to the "Creek rebellion." He made prisoners of the chiefs and leaders who had protested the US takeover of their land. Finally, in 1836, the Creek people were ordered

Mistippe, 13-year-old Creek boy, traveled with his father, Yoholo-Micco, to Washington where he had this portrait painted. White officials there could not believe Mistippe's skill with a blowgun. He showed them how he could snuff out a candle in four out of five shots and bring down a bird with a single shot. The blowgun (above), the Creeks' favorite hunting weapon, was a reed several feet long. The arrow was made of light wood, the point barbed and thistledown wrapped on the other end. One US official who tried the blowgun said it had the speed and accuracy of a rifle ball.

out of Alabama. Over 14,000 Creeks, some of their chiefs in chains, were forcibly moved to the land assigned to them in the area now called Oklahoma.

Famous Creeks

ALEXANDER MCGILLIVRAY: Alexander McGillivray [muh-GILL-vree], chief of the Creeks from 1783 to 1793, ranks as one of the most influential of the Southern Indian leaders. A highly skilled diplomat, he knew how to barter with the colonial powers, how to play France, England, Spain, and the United States against each other for the benefit of the Creeks.

His father, Lachlan McGillivray, was a Scottish trader, who first exchanged a jackknife for rabbit skins. Lachlan married a half-blooded Creek woman, Sehoy Marchand of the powerful Wind Clan. They lived at Little Tallassee in Alabama where Alexander was born in 1759. His Indian name was Hippo-ilk-micco, "the good child king."

When he was twelve, Alexander was sent to Charleston to an English school. He became the best educated Indian of his time. The letters he wrote on behalf of the Creek Nation are the earliest written records we have by a Southern Indian. All other papers concerning tribal affairs were written by whites. Like most Indians of mixed blood, McGillivray's loyalty was always to the tribe. He served the Creeks with unusual ability because he knew both the world of the Indian and the world of the white man.

At the height of his power, McGillivray traveled to New York City to meet with President George Washington on tribal business. McGillivray made the journey on horseback and in wagons, with his nephew and two attendants. He had the distinction of riding up Wall Street by Washington's side.

When McGillivray died in Pensacola on February 17, 1793. a London paper, which noted the deaths of royalty and distinguished international persons, carried the notice of the death of the Alabama Indian chief.

MARY BOSOMWORTH: General James Oglethorpe gave a diamond ring and a large sum of money to a Creek woman, Coosaponakeesa [coo-sah-poh-nah-KEE-sah], to thank her for the help she had given him in founding the Georgia colony. The woman is know to us as Mary Musgrove Matthews Bosomworth.

Mary was no ordinary Creek, but the niece of the powerful Creek chief known as Emperor Brims. She was born in 1700 at Coweta in the Creek country. Her English names come from the three white men she married.

Educated at an English school in Charleston, Mary served as an interpreter—explaining what each was saying when Indian and white men talked to each other. Oglethorpe appointed her his interpreter and agent with the Indians, paying her $500 a year. She interpreted all of Oglethorpe's speeches and helped draw up and settle treaties.

Largely because of Mary Bosomworth, who held the high position of Beloved Woman in the tribe, the Creeks in Colonial times remained friendly to the British and held back the Spanish who were pushing from Florida. For many years Mary operated trading posts, and she reported to Oglethorpe what she heard from both her Indian and her white customers.

The story of Mary Bosomworth might be different had she not married, at age forty-nine, a former clergyman named Thomas Bosomworth. He took on as a full-time job the management of Mary's lands. But he turned out to be an adventurer, out to get all he could for himself. He persuaded Mary to declare herself Empress of the Creeks and to demand that the colony of Georgia return to her the land that had been given her by the Creeks.

When the British refused, Mary gathered a large force of Creek warriors and marched on Savannah. She was in Indian dress and her husband was wearing clerical robes as they led the warriors, painted for battle, into the city. They were met by a troop of cavalry and forced to put down their weapons.

The Indians met with the city council for several days. The council convinced the Indians—but not Mary and Thomas—that she had no claim to the lands. The Indians were given presents and sent home. Mary and Thomas were put in jail until they agreed to stop making trouble.

Later Mary went to England to plead her cause. Finally, after many lawsuits, she was given a grant to the Island of St. Catherine off the Georgia coast. She died there in 1763.

MENAWA: Menawa [MEN-uh-wuh] was a powerful chief of the Upper Creeks who lived at Okfuskee (Alabama). He was born about 1766 on the Tallapoosa River. As a young

Menawa, Creek war chief, received seven bullet wounds at Horseshoe Bend and was passed over for dead on the battlefield. Reviving after dark, he made his way to the river's edge and escaped by canoe. The portrait, appearing in the Mckenney-Hall Portrait Gallery of American Indians, was painted by Charles Bird King in 1826.

man he earned the name Hothlepoya, Crazy War Hunter, because of daring raids he made on the Tennessee border.

By the early 1800s Menawa was no longer called Crazy War Hunter. He had become Menawa, Great Warrior. When the Creeks split into Upper and Lower Creeks, Menawa became a war chief of the Upper Creeks.

In the Creek Indian War, the Upper Creeks under Menawa fought to keep their homeland intact, but they were no match for the forces of Andrew Jackson. They made a final stand at the Battle of the Horseshoe. Menawa won lasting fame in Indian history at this battle. A prophet or medicine man of the Upper Creeks, Monehell, claimed to have foreseen Jackson's battle plan. Because his power was greater than Menawa's, he directed the defense of the Horseshoe. When his prophecies proved wrong, and many warriors had died, the enraged Menawa turned on the prophet and slew him. He then took command of the Indian forces and with a thunderous cry plunged into battle.

In the action that followed, Menawa received seven bullet wounds and was passed over for dead on the battlefield. When he regained consciousness that night, he crawled to the river, pulled himself into a canoe and was carried downstream. A group of Creek women, hiding with the children away from the battle, saw the canoe and rescued Menawa. He recovered from his wounds but remained scarred for the rest of his life.

Menawa returned to Okfuskee and resumed his position as chief of the Upper Creek towns. He continued to oppose cession of Creek lands. When William McIntosh illegally signed the Indian Springs Treaty in 1825, deeding all of Creek lands in Georgia to the United States, the Creek council decided McIntosh must die a traitor's death. They selected Menawa to lead the warriors in executing him.

In 1826, with a group of Creek leaders, Menawa went to Washington to protest the Indian Springs Treaty. The Creeks signed a new treaty about which Menawa said, "I have smoked the pipe of peace with my Great Father, and have buried the tomahawk so deep it cannot be dug up." It was on this visit that Charles Byrd King painted Menawa's portrait. Menawa agreed to sit if he could have a copy of the portrait.

In 1836 Menawa offered his services to the state of Alabama in the Seminole War. He joined forces with Opothle-Yaholo, a former Lower Creek enemy, to quell revolting Creeks and Seminoles in Florida. He wore the uniform of a US officer.

Because he had fought on the side of the United States, Menawa expected that his request to remain on his ancestral lands in Alabama would be granted. Some Creeks had been allowed this privilege. But when he returned from the Seminole War, he found his land and possessions gone, and his family moved west. Now almost 70 years old, he had no choice but to leave his homeland and join his family across the Mississippi.

Before he departed he visited a white friend, presenting him with the copy of his portrait. He said: "I am going away. I have brought you this picture. I wish you to take it and hang it up in your house. When your children look at it, you can tell them what I have been. Great as my regard for you is, I never wish to see you in that new country . . . for when I cross the great river, my desire is that I may never again see the face of a white man."

There is no record of his life in the new country, not even when and where he died. His granddaughter, Hannah Monahwee, was head of a school in the Creek Nation in Oklahoma in 1894.

WILLIAM MCINTOSH: William McIntosh, head chief of the powerful Lower Creek town of Coweta (Alabama) from 1800 to 1825, played an important role in Creek history as an ally of the United States.

In the Creek Indian War, at the Battle of Horseshoe Bend, McIntosh commanded the Lower Creek Indians fighting on the side of the United States. He was one of the signers of the treaty that ended the Creek Indian War. Later, McIntosh fought with General Andrew Jackson in Florida against the Seminoles. He was commissioned a

When the US Government sent two commissioners to persuade the Creeks to give up more land, Opothle-Yaholo[oh-POTH-leh-yah-H OE-loe] on February 8, 1825, addressed the treaty council at Indian Springs, Georgia: "Leave us what little we have. We sell no more. Let us die where our fathers died. Let us sleep where our kindred sleep." But Opothle-Yaholo's speech did no good. The chief went west with his people in 1836.

general and placed in charge of all Indian troops in Florida. After the Seminole War, McIntosh returned to Georgia and became a wealthy cotton planter, owning many slaves.

But McIntosh's fate was sealed when he signed away Creek land at the Treaty of Indian Springs in 1825. Just the year before, the Creek national council had voted that any Creek who signed away land would be put to death. At that meeting Opothle-Yaholo had pointed his finger at McIntosh and said: "I have told you your fate if you sign that paper. I once more say, beware!" After McIntosh signed the treaty, Menawa led a party of Upper Creeks to McIntosh's home to avenge the signing. The raiders attacked at dawn, set fire to the house, and shot McIntosh. They considered him a traitor to the Creek nation.

We can understand this incident if we remember that no individual Indian—not even a chief—had the right to sell or sign away land. Land belonged to the tribe—all the people— and only by tribal action could it be sold or ceded.

WILLIAM WEATHERFORD: William Weatherford, or Red Eagle, an important leader in the Creek Indian War, was born in 1765 into the powerful Wind Clan. His father, a Scottish trader, married a half-sister of Alexander McGillivray (see p. 91) and settled down to operate a trading post in the heart of Creek country at Coosada (Alabama). Here young Weatherford came under the influence of his powerful uncle. He made journeys with McGillivray on the diplomatic missions, trying to keep Creek land from white settlers.

After McGillivray's death, Weatherford saw no hope that the Creeks could keep their land by peaceful means. He led the attack by Creek warriors on white settlers at Fort Mims in 1813. In retaliation whites pursued the Creeks to the Holy Ground. Weatherford barely escaped. Legend says that he rode his horse, Arrow, to a bluff on the nearby river. Still on horseback he leaped from the bluff and plunged into the water far below. His pursuers never saw him or his horse surface and gave them up for dead.

At the Battle of Horseshoe Bend, Andrew Jackson broke the resistance of the Upper Creeks. He ordered that all the

Creek leaders be brought to him, but Red Eagle could not be found. A few days later Red Eagle walked alone into Jackson's camp and offered his life in exchange for the lives of his people. He said: "Jackson, I am not afraid of you. I fear no man, for I am a Creek warrior. I have nothing to request in behalf of myself; you can kill me, if you desire. But I come to beg you to send for the women and children of the war party, who are now starving in the woods. Their fields and cribs have been destroyed by your people, who have driven them to the woods without an ear of corn. I hope that you will send out parties, who will safely conduct them here, in order that they may be fed. I exerted myself in vain to prevent the massacre of the women and children at Fort Mims. I am now done fighting. The Red Sticks are nearly all killed. My warriors can no longer hear my voice: their bones are at Talladega, Tallushatchee, Emuckfaw, and Tohopeka. I rely upon your generosity."

Impressed with Red Eagle's bravery, Jackson sent him away a free man. Red Eagle moved to south Alabama where he farmed until his death in 1826.

After the crushing defeat suffered by the Creeks at Horseshoe Bend, the Creek leader William Weatherford (Red Eagle) walked alone into Jackson's Camp. In this old engraving he is shown pleading with Jackson to rescue the Creek women and children in the woods.

Tribal council members of the Poarch Band of the Creek Naton East of the Mississippi, 1982 (left to right): John Arthur McGhee, Buford Rolin and Eddie Tullis (chairman).

Brothers: We have heard the talk of our Great Father; it is very kind. He says he loves his red children.

When the first white man came over the wide waters, he was but a little man ... very little. His legs were cramped by sitting long in his big boat, and he begged for a little land.

When he came to these shores the Indians gave him land, and kindled fires to make him comfortable.

But when the white man had warmed himself at the Indian's fire, and had filled himself with the Indian's hominy, he became very large. He stopped not at the mountain tops, and his foot covered the plains and the valleys. His hands grasped the eastern and western seas. Then he became our Great Father. He loved his red children, but he said: "You must move a little farther, lest by accident I tread on you."

Now he says, "The land you live upon is not yours. Go beyond the Mississippi; there is game; there you may remain while the grass grows and the rivers run."

Will not our Great Father come there also? He loves his red children, and his tongue is not forked.

Brothers! I have listened to a great many talks from our Great Father. But they always began and ended in this—'Get a little farther; you are too near me." I have spoken.

SPECKLED SNAKE, aged Creek chief, spoke in 1829, one year before the Indian Removal Act, which gave President Andrew Jackson the authority to move all the Southern tribes west of the Mississippi.

Sounds and Meanings

Creek Place Names Used Today

Name and location	How to pronounce name	What it means
Apalachicola, Fla.	a-puh-lah-chih-KOE-lah	People who live on the other side of a stream.
Altamaha River, Ga.	al-tuh-MAH-ha	Way to the Tama country. Tama was an Indian town where the Oconee and Ocmulgee Rivers flow together to make the Altamaha.
Atoka, Tenn.	ah-TOE-kuh	Ball ground.
Chattahoochee River	cha-tuh-HOO-chee	Marked rocks. Pictured rocks are found in the riverbed.
Chunnenuggee, Ala.	chuh-neh-NUH-gee	Long ridge.
Coagie Creek, Ala.	KOE-gee	Cane noise—from the sound of wind in the cane.
Dahlonega, Ga.	dah-LON-eh-guh	Yellow metal or yellow gold.
Notasulga, Ala.	noe-tah-SULL-gah	Many teeth. So named perhaps because of teeth found there.
Okefenokee, Ga.	OH-kee-feh-NO-kee	Trembling water.
Opelika, Ala.	oh-peh-LYE-kuh	Big swamp.
Palatka, Ga.	puh-LAT-kuh	Boat crossing.
Patsaliga Creek, Ala.	pat-suh-LYE-guh	Pigeon roosting place.
Penholoway Creek, Ga.	pen-ho-LOE-way	Foot-log high. Where an Indian trail crossed the stream on a fallen tree.
Talladega, Ala.	tal-uh-DEH-guh	Boarder town. Located between the lands of the Creeks and the Natchez.
Towaliga River, Ga.	toe-uh-LYE-guh	Scalp place, Probably a spot where war parties halted to dry scalps.
Tullahoma, Tenn.	tuh-luh-HOME-uh	Red town.
Wallahatchee Creek, Ala.	wah-lah-HATCH-ee	War-divider creek. Name indicated that this village announced the opening of a war.
Wetumpka, Ala.	weh-TUM-kah	Tumbling water.

The number seven was sacred to the Cherokees. In the tribe there were seven clans; every town included people from all seven. This cutsom linked the Cherokee nation in bonds of kinship. The council house was seven-sided so each clan could sit together. The Cherokees believed there were seven directions– north, south, east, west, up , down, and where one was.

7

Cherokees,
the Principal
People

A dramatic incident that took place in 1838 guaranteed a place in history for a man named Tsali.

At that time the US Government was trying, with great difficulty, to round up the Cherokees in preparation for moving them to unsettled land in the west. A few tribal leaders, against the wishes of most of their people, had signed away the ancient Cherokee homeland for "safe passage" to an unknown territory.

Tsali and his wife, along with some relatives, had been seized by General Winfield Scott's soldiers. But Tsali's feeble wife was unable to keep up, and when a soldier prodded her with his bayonet, the Cherokees turned on the soldiers, killing one of them, and escaped into the mountains.

Meanwhile, hundreds of other Cherokees were also escaping from the stockades the Government had built to hold them. They had fled into remote mountain areas and were defying all attempts at capture. Hearing about the incident in which Tsali's men had killed one of his soldiers, General Scott realized he had a bargaining point. Through a white man who was a friend of the Cherokees, he persuaded Tsali to surrender on condition that the rest of the tribe be allowed to remain in their mountain homes.

So it was that Tsali, his brother, and his three sons were shot by a firing squad of General Scott's soldiers. Tsali's

The Cherokees' skin tends to be olive in color, lighter than the coppery "red skin" of the Southern tribes. Their hair is straight and black and their noses long and pointed. The portrait is of Tah-chee, a chief.

youngest son, Wasituna (Washington), was spared because of his youth.

In spite of Tsali's sacrifice, only about a thousand Cherokees managed to remain in their mountain homeland. Nevertheless, the Cherokees survived the ordeal of removal from the South. Far from being "vanishing Americans," the tribe now outnumbers the Cherokee population when the whites first met them. Today 50,000 live in Oklahoma, and about 5,000 in North Carolina.

We probably know more about the Cherokees than any other Southern tribe, because of their large numbers and because of their long contact with white people. They were the largest tribe in the South, and one of the largest in all of North America. They made more treaties with the United States Government than any other tribe. Christian missionaries worked among them for over a hundred years.

The Cherokees called themselves the "principal people." The name *Cherokee*, meaning "people of a different speech," was given them by the other Southern tribes who belonged to a different language family. The Cherokees were the only large Southern tribe not belonging to the Muskogean language family; their language was Iroquoian.

The Cherokees believed that far back in their history the Iroquois had been their brothers. According to legend, the brothers separated just after crossing a large body of water, the Cherokees went south, the Iroquois north. It is a fact that the Cherokees slowly migrated southward until they finally stopped and settled in what is now western North Carolina.

The Cherokees and the Whites

The Spanish explorer De Soto visited Cherokee country in 1540. At one town Indian leaders came out to greet him in fur robes and feathered headdresses. Gold mines lured other Spaniards before 1600.

The British came in 1690, also seeking gold. By 1700 the Cherokees had been given firearms by the British, who wanted their friendship. The Cherokees now became a force to reckon with in the frontier wars of the white man and in the tribal wars between Indians. The Cherokees succeeded in driving the Tuscaroras from the Carolinas and the Shawnees out of the Cumberland River region of present-day Tennessee. They defeated the Creeks for the possession of upper Georgia.

In the French and Indian War of 1756 England built three forts in Cherokee country. The Cherokees sided with the British in the beginning, but when British soldiers and white frontiersman mistreated the Cherokees, their war chief Oconostota rebelled.

Attakullakulla [att-koola-koola], a great chief of the Cherokees, stopped the fighting and in 1763 journeyed to Augusta, Georgia, where the chiefs of the Southern tribes met to sign a peace treaty with the British. Within a few years the Cherokees had given up large tracts of their land by treaties. Attakullakulla's son Dragging Canoe resisted the takeover of Indian lands by whites. He led a large band of warriors and their families southwest. They built a new tribal settlement on Chickamauga Creek near present-day Chattanooga and became known as the Chickamaugas, the most warlike of the Cherokees. Spurred on by the British, Dragging Canoe's forces raided white settlements bordering Cherokee country.

As the Cherokees met more and more white people;

These Cherokee chiefs accompanied Alexander Cuming to London in 1730. At far right is Atakullakulla, then a youth.

they began to take on white people's ways. They also became victims of European diseases. In the mid-1700s smallpox killed almost half of the Cherokee population.

Many Cherokees gave up their hunting life as they tried to imitate the white man's way of life. The US Government furnished the Cherokees with farming tools, spinning wheels and looms. Spinning and weaving became a major industry in many Cherokee homes by 1820. The coat or shirt of striped homespun woolen cloth became a distinctive part of Cherokee dress. But even as they farmed and spun, the Cherokees kept alive many old tribal customs. They continued to live in villages and towns built around central squares. Each town was surrounded by fields where corn, potatoes, and beans were grown. In 1775 there were forty such towns. Women continued the old arts of making baskets and pottery. Men still hunted, selling pelts to white traders. Like other Southern Indians, the Cherokees played stickball and chunkey (see pp. 54 and 86). Both men and women played a dice-like game using painted beads.

It was in trying to be like the white people that Sequoyah in 1821 perfected his plan for writing the Cherokee language. (See p. 109.) Within three years many Cherokees learned to read and write their own language. With the help of missionaries they published at New Echota a newspaper in both

Cherokee and English. The newspaper, *The Cherokee Phoenix*, aroused interest around the world, for the Cherokees were the only Indian tribe to have their own press.

By 1830 the Cherokees had formed a system of government modeled on that of the United States. They adopted a constitution and set up a legislature with upper and lower houses. The legislature, called the general council, had the power to elect a president or principal chief.

How the Cherokees Lost Their Land

The Cherokees may have thought that learning the white man's ways would help them survive as a nation. But they quickly learned that they were only pawns in the Europeans' fight for control of the New World, and that the white people wanted their tribal lands.

When the Revolutionary War began, the Cherokees took the side of the British against the colonists. The result was that they were not only on the losing side, but by 1791 had lost to the US much of their land in North and South Carolina and east Tennessee.

Still the Cherokees continued learning the ways of the white people and adapting themselves to a new and different lifestyle. In spite of the loss of land, the Cherokee Nation reached the height of its development (at least, in terms of white civilization) under John Ross, the chief elected in 1828. Ross was one-eighth Cherokee, of Scottish descent, but he considered himself all Indian. He brought lawsuits against the state of Georgia and the US Government, trying to keep tribal lands. But it proved to be a losing battle. When gold was discovered near Dahlonega, Georgia, on Cherokee land, whites rushed into the area. Andrew Jackson, the former Indian fighter who was now President of the United States, sided with the state of Georgia.

The US Supreme Court in 1831 upheld Georgia's claim to Cherokee lands. This decision increased the determination of whites to move the Cherokees away from the South.

The Cherokee Nation itself was split over the question

of removal. John Ross continued to plead with the Government for Indian rights. But Major Ridge and his son John felt further resistance was useless. They saw a removal treaty as the only way out of a desperate situation.

The climax came in 1835 with the Treaty of New Echota. US agents, with the help of Major and John Ridge, persuaded a small group of Cherokees to sign away all Cherokee lands and to move west of the Mississippi River. Fewer than 500 Cherokees (out of a population of 17,000) were present at the meeting. None of the officers of the Cherokee Nation signed the treaty.

John Ross and white leaders Henry Clay, Daniel Webster, and David Crockett tried to revoke the treaty, but they failed. Eight million acres of Cherokee land became the property of the United States, at about 50 cents an acre. Soon after, 40-acre tracts in the gold field in Georgia were sold for as much as $30,000 by white speculators.

The Trail of Tears

The Cherokee Trail of Tears was actually three routes. One route used rivers—the Tennessee, the Mississippi, and the Arkansas.

In May 1838 the forced removal, known to the Cherokees as the Trail of Tears, began. John Ridge, with his family and

about 2,000 followers, had already left for the territory in the west assigned to them by the US Government. The rest of the people, under Chief Ross, remained, still hopeful that they would not have to move. The US sent General Winfield Scott to round them up.

In Cherokee, North Carolina, Cherokees of today sit in front of the council house where tribal affairs are conducted.

Ross persuaded Scott to let the Cherokees manage their own removal. He divided the 13,000 people into groups of a thousand. They started their 800-mile journey late in October, most of them on foot. The cold weather, illness, and lack of proper food caused more than 4,000 Cherokees to die on the long march. Those who survived reached Oklahoma in the early spring of 1839.

In June Major and John Ridge were killed by newly arrived Cherokees who felt they had disobeyed tribal law by selling tribal land back in the east. Chief Ross denied any connection with the murders, but his followers were said to be responsible.

The Cherokees who live today on the Qualla reservation in North Carolina are descendants of Tsali and the other Cherokees who hid in the mountains during the roundup of 1838. Later the North Carolina Cherokees were granted citizenship and allowed to purchase land, bringing into being the Qualla Boundary (reservation) in southwest North Carolina.

Famous Cherokees

JOHN ROSS: Blue-eyed and fair-skinned John Ross may not have looked like an Indian, but he was a great Cherokee leader at the most crucial time in his tribe's history. The Cherokees elected him to be their head chief as they fought to stay on their land.

Ross was born at Turkey Town, an Indian village in Alabama, in 1790. His father, a Scottish trader, sent him to a white school in Tennessee. When Ross was nineteen, an agent of the United States sent him on a mission to the Cherokees in Arkansas. From that time until his death Ross served the Cherokee Nation.

In the Creek Indian War he commanded a Cherokee regiment that fought against the Creeks. From 1819 to 1826 he was president of the Cherokee National Council. When the Cherokees set up a new government in 1828 Ross was elected principal chief, a position like that of President of the United States.

Ross worked hard to develop programs to train the Cherokees in practical skills. He made many trips to Washington to defend the rights of his people before Congress and President Jackson. He could not believe that the Cherokees, always friendly to the United States, would be forced from their homeland. When US soldiers came to round up the Cherokees, Ross finally admitted defeat. The sad task of leading his people from their homes fell to him. His wife died along with 4,000 other Cherokees on the Trail of Tears.

In the new territory John Ross continued to lead his people. Once again he was elected principal chief, this time of the United Cherokee Nation in its new capital at Tahlequah, Oklahoma.

He died in Washington in 1866 while working on a treaty to continue the Cherokee government.

John Ross, Cherokee chief.

SEQUOYAH: Sequoyah made a unique contribution to history when singlehandedly he devised a written language for the Cherokees. His achievement made this the only tribe in America to have a written language. The great sequoia trees of California are named in honor of this man.

Sequoyah was born about 1750 to a white trader and a Cherokee woman. He watched white people reading, and he came to believe it was the "talking leaves" (the papers they read) that gave them their power. To enable the Cherokees also to talk to each other in writing, he began making an alphabet. He gave so much time and thought to developing a written Cherokee language that he neglected his other work (he was a silversmith and a blacksmith) and his family. His friends and neighbors thought he was crazy. His wife accused him of witchcraft, and the Cherokee Nation tried him for witchcraft. Although he was not convicted, his wife received permission to set fire to the cabin where he was working on the alphabet. The loss of his cabin only spurred him on, and he went back to work.

Finally in 1821 Sequoyah completed a system for writing the Cherokee language, a system that was simple enough for all the people to learn. At first the Cherokee Council rejected its use. Then they changed their mind. The art of writing spread like wildfire through Cherokee country.

In 1827 the newspaper *The Cherokee Phoenix* began publication in both Cherokee and English. It carried information for Cherokee farmers on cattle raising, food processing, and dairying. The press also published portions of the Bible, hymnbooks, and laws passed by the council.

Sequoyah went to Arkansas in 1822 to teach his alphabet to the Cherokees who had moved west. He also made many trips to Washington, D.C. He died in 1843 in New Mexico while looking for a band of lost Cherokees.

In developing his syllabary—85 symbols representing all the sounds in the Cherokee language—Sequoyah became the only known person to invent an alphabet without being able to read or write any other language.

NANCY WARD: Nancy Ward, one of the best-known women in Indian history, was the last Beloved Woman of the Cherokees. She played an important role in keeping peace between her people and the white settlers.

Her Cherokee name was Nanye-hi, meaning "One Who Goes About." The settlers changed this name to Nancy because it was easier for them to say.

She was born in 1738 in the Cherokee capital, Echota (near today's Madisonville in east Tennessee). Her uncle was the powerful Chief Attakullakulla. In the 1750s Nancy married and went with her husband to Georgia to fight the Creeks who were claiming Cherokee land. In the battle, after her husband was killed, Nancy took charge and led the Cherokees to victory. Although not yet twenty years old, Nancy was selected by the Cherokees to be a Beloved Woman. In this role she headed the Council of Women and voted in the Chief's Council. She could also decide the fate of any captive and speak her opinion on all matters of tribal concern.

Nancy's second marriage was to an Irishman named Bryant Ward. He was a trader among the Cherokees and had fought against the British. No doubt Nancy was influenced by him in her friendly feelings toward white people. She believed that the Cherokees had to learn the ways of the white people and to live with them in peace.

When Cherokees moved to attack a white settlement, Nancy sent a warning to the settlers. One of the white women was captured and brought to the Indian camp to be put to death. But Nancy, using her power as a Beloved Woman, refused to allow the execution. The warriors obeyed and set the woman free.

In the War for Independence the colonists' troops marched into Cherokee country because the Cherokees had sided with the British. Nancy was sent by the chiefs to meet them and try to stop them. But Cherokee land was laid waste. More than a thousand cabins were burned and 50,000 bushels of corn destroyed. At the war's end, however, the Cherokees were the first tribe to pledge allegiance to the United States.

When George Washington became President he made it

clear that he wanted peace with the Indians. He sent a peace commission to meet the Indians in South Carolina in 1785. At the meeting Nancy, still stately and beautiful, spoke for her people. "I hope that you have now taken us by the hand in real friendship. I have borne and raised up warriors. I am now old, but hope yet to bear children who will grow up and people our Nation now that we are under the protection of Congress and shall have no more disturbance. The young warriors rejoice that we have peace and hope that the chain of friendship will never be broken."

In the following years Nancy prospered. She opened an inn on Lake Ocoee (Tennessee) where travelers liked to stop. She owned slaves and livestock and lived, surrounded by her family, in a well-furnished home.

The white settlers affectionately called her Granny Ward. She is buried in Benton, Tennessee, and her grave is marked by a bronze tablet reading: "Princess and Prophetess of Tennessee. The Pocahontas of Tennessee and the Constant Friend of the American Pioneer."

MAJOR RIDGE AND JOHN RIDGE: To some Cherokees Major Ridge was a hero because he moved them west before the Trail of Tears. To other Cherokees he was a traitor because he sold Cherokee land without the consent of the Cherokee Council.

Major Ridge, his son John Ridge, and Elias Boudinot, the editor of the Cherokee newspaper, were killed by other Cherokees after they had moved west. Major Ridge's enemies considered the deaths justified; he had disobeyed tribal law, which said Indian land belonged to all the tribe.

Major Ridge

Born about 1771 on the Hiwassee River in present-day Polk County, Tennessee, Major Ridge was given the name Path Killer. At age fourteen he joined his first war party to fight the white settlers. For years after that he opposed US Government plans to send the Cherokees west. He urged his people to learn the white man's ways, to improve their farming methods, to build roads, and to establish a government based on that of the United States. He believed that if they did these things they would be allowed to stay on their land. But as the US refused time after time to protect the Cherokees' rights, Ridge changed his mind. He eventually signed the Treaty of New Echota, giving up all Cherokee land. The signing of this treaty brought about a split in the Cherokee Nation, a division which never healed even after the tribe moved west.

John Ridge believed, as his father did, that the only way for the Cherokee Nation to survive was to move west. He saw that whiskey was turning warriors into drunkards, that fields were being neglected, and that white settlers were moving onto Indian lands. He made plans for the removal of the Cherokee people through the Cherokee newspaper *The Cherokee Phoenix*.

Both Major Ridge and John Ridge made many trips to Washington to plead the cause of their people with the President and the Congress.

Sounds and Meanings

Cherokee Place Names Used Today

Name and location	How to pronounce	What it means
Ahaluna Gap, N.C.	ah-hah-LOO-nah	Place where they were ambushed. Cherokees used the place for a lookout; here they ambushed a party of invading Iroquois.
Attala, Miss. and Attalla, Ala.		Mountain.
Chattanooga, Tenn.	CHAT-uh-NOO-guh	Rock rising to a point. Probably refers to Lookout Mountain.
Cheowa, N.C.	chee-owe-uh	Otter place.
Cowee, N.C.	COE-ee	Deer clan place.
Cullowhee, N.C.	cull-oh-hee	Place of the spring salad.
Etowah, Ga.	EH-toe-wuh	Deadwood place.
Nantahala Gorge, N.C.	nan-tuh-HAY-luh	Land of the middle sun. The gorge was so deep only the midday sun could penetrate its depths.
Oothkalooga Creek, Ga.	OOTH-kuh-LOO-guh	Beaver dam.
Sahkanaga, N.C.	sah-kah-nah-gah	The great blue hills of God—the name the Cherokees gave the Blue Ridge Mountains.
Santeetlah Lake, N.C.	san-TEET-luh	Blue waters.
Screamer Mountain, Ga.		Named for a Cherokee who broke away from the roundup of his tribe during the Removal and fled screaming to the mountains.
Tennessee		First the name of a Cherokee town, then the name given to a small stream nearby. As the settlers moved westward, downstream, they carried the name along until the stream became a large river, the Tennessee.
Tesnatee, Ga.	tess-nah-tee	Wild turkey.
Unaka Mountain, Tenn.	oo-nah-kah	White. A white haze often crowns the summit.

Osceola, the most famous Seminole, achieved lasting fame in American history when he chose death in a South Carolina prison rather than surrender to US authorities. He is pictured here in a hunting skirt. A turban of red cloth with three ostrich plumes circles his head. Hanging from his neck are three silver gorgets which Osceola wore in all of his portraits.

8

Seminoles,
A People Who
Never Surrendered

The Seminoles did not even exist as a tribe until about the time of the American Revolution. This fact makes them different from the four other main tribes of the South.

Small groups of Indians drifted into the area now called Florida from Alabama and Georgia. Some came to get away from white settlers, others to escape tribal wars, and still others because the hunting was good. Whatever the reasons, they left the Creek Confederacy behind and gradually came together to form the Seminole tribe. Their name comes from a word meaning "the wild (free) ones."

Most of the original Florida Indians had been killed by the Spaniards or sold by them into slavery in Cuba and the West Indies. The few who survived later joined the Seminoles. Runaway black slaves hid out with the Seminoles and many became tribal members. After the Battle of Horseshoe Bend in Alabama in 1814, as many as 2,500 Creeks fled south and joined the Seminoles.

Trouble with the Whites

The Seminoles lived first in north Florida around today's Tallahassee. The land was rich, and they farmed and hunted. Some raised horses and cattle.

Seminole warriors used their knowledge of Florida swamps to hide from US soldiers and then come out and ambush small groups. They were masters of guerrilla warfare.

The white settlers in the region were angry because the Seminoles protected black slaves and because the Seminoles had sided with the British in the American Revolution. In the War of 1812 the US Army entered Seminole country to keep the Indians from joining the British.

The white settlers were angry also because they wanted the land the Seminoles lived on. In 1821, when the United States bought Florida from Spain, whites wasted no time in claiming Seminole land.

In 1823 the Seminoles were forced to give up 32 million acres of fine farmland for a 4-million acre reservation in central Florida. Their new home was not suited for farming. The people became hungry and raided white settlements. As more and more settlers pushed into Florida, the United

States said all Indians must go to the new territory set aside for them west of the Mississippi River. Black slaves who had joined the tribe and married Indians must be left behind.

Most of the Seminoles refused to leave, and another Seminole war broke out. For seven years the Seminoles resisted armed forces sent against them by the US Government. Finally, in 1833, a few chiefs bribed by the whites agreed to the Payne's Landing Treaty and signed away all Seminole land for territory west of the Mississippi. The treaty tore the tribe apart. Many Seminoles went west, but others fled into the swamps of the Everglades in south Florida. US troops followed them, but the Seminoles moved deeper and deeper into the swamps and eluded them. Their descendants live there today.

Life in the Everglades

In the Everglades the Seminoles found a whole new way of life. Instead of log cabins they built open huts thatched with palm leaves, which were cooler and blended into the swamp growth.

They became a boat people because there were no foot trails to follow in the swamp. The white men could not find them. Staying hidden in their villages, the Seminoles did not learn white ways or the English language.

The swamp villages were small, only a few houses to a hummock (mound) of dry land. The houses were called chickees. The chickee was built about three feet off the ground, open on every side, and with a palm-leaf roof. The family slept on mats on the floor.

Each family did its cooking over a big open fire in the center of the village. Coontie was a favorite food made from the roots of a swamp plant; cakes were made from flour pounded from the plant.

Sofkee, a soupy dish made from cornmeal, was always a part of a Seminole meal. The Seminoles used palm leaves or shells to hold their food. They also used shells for knives and garden hoes.

Seminoles lived in open-sided thatch-roof houses called chickees. Chickee floors were raised several feet off the ground for protection against the dampness of the Everglade swamps. The palm tree native to south Florida furnished materials for building the chickee: wood from the trunk for poles and palm branches for the roof. This drawing was made about 1885 by Clay MacCauley to illustrate Seminole Indian life for the Bureau of American Ethnology.

Seminoles dressed in a different way from other Southern Indians, more like the Indians of Peru. Buckskin, which the Creeks wore, was too warm for the Florida climate. The Seminoles traded with the whites for cotton cloth which they made into loose-fitting garments. The women wore skirts to the ground and cape-like blouses. The men wore long shirts down to their knees. In spite of the warm climate, they had to protect their bodies from mosquitoes and other insects and from the sharp-edged grasses and spiny plants of the Everglades.

With the coming of the sewing machine, Seminole dress became more colorful. Bits of cloth were sewed together in patchwork designs. As many as 5,000 small pieces of cloth might be in a skirt. Colorful braid was also sewed around the skirt. Women wore heavy strings of beads around the neck like high collars. The men wore bandannas and turbans with plumes.

Seminoles live in Florida today on reservations. You can see them along the Tamiami Trail through the Everglades. Some still live in chickees and make a living in shops selling to tourists. Many have left the swamps to be a part of modern Florida. Yet they are still Seminoles, proud to be a people who never surrendered.

Sewing machines became the proud possessions of Seminole women, enabling them to make gaily decorated , multicolored, and braided dresses and jackets. Seminole women did not consider themselves well-dressed without many strands of colored beads around their necks.

A Seminole woman of today cooks bread in a building something like the chickee. Her dress, in contrast to that of the young woman beside her, is in the colorful and traditional style of her tribe.

The Seminoles have their tribal headquarters at Hollywood Seminole Reservation. Here one can visit a village featuring typical Indian customs, arts, and crafts. There are also four other reservations in Florida: Brighton Reservation in Glades County, home of the Creek Seminoles; Big Cypress Reservation in Hendry County, Miccosukee Seminoles; Florida State Reservation, set aside for Miccosukees and Seminoles as a hunting and fishing area; and Miccosukee Reservation in Dade County. (The Miccosukees are politically separate from the Seminoles, although they are of the same stock. The Miccosukees would not sign the treaty of 1837, which was agreed to by the Seminoles. They became a breakaway group, continuing their traditional tribal religion, while the Seminoles adopted the Christian religion.)

Famous Seminoles

OSCEOLA: Osceola [oh-see-OH-la] was the most famous Seminole and one of the best known of all Indians. He was born on the Tallapoosa River in the Creek country about 1810. His mother was a Creek and his father a half-breed Scot. Legend says that at the Battle of Horseshoe Bend his mother covered her young son's body with her own and they were passed over for dead.

With the power of the Creek Nation broken, Osceola moved with his family to Florida. He grew up to become a leader of his people. He respected the rights of the black people who had come to live with the Seminoles. Many of the blacks were former slaves; Osceola refused to send them back to their white masters.

Osceola dared to defy the US Army when it came to try to move the Seminoles west, and he refused to sign a treaty giving up the last of Seminole lands. He drew his knife and stabbed it through the treaty papers. "This land is ours," he said. "This is the way we will sign all such treaties. You have guns; so have we. Your men will fight and so will ours—till the last drop of Seminole blood has moistened the dust of his hunting ground."

In 1834 Osceola led his people into the Everglades to hide. Two years later, under a flag of truce while meeting with US Army officers, he was tricked and taken prisoner. He was sent in chains with his wife and children to Fort Moultrie, South Carolina, in September 1837. Placed in a dark prison, he refused to eat. In January 1838, still a young man, he died.

Osceola sat for this portrait shortly before he died in prison. George Catlin was the painter. Since magazines and newspapers depended on artists for pictures (there were no photographers in 1837), several other artists also sketched Osceola.

Osceola draws his knife and pins the treaty paper to the table, crying, "This land is ours. This is the way I will sign all such treaties." This incident occurred at Fort King, Florida.

Walt Whitman, after reading newspaper accounts of the death of Osceola, wrote:

When his hour for death had come,
He slowly raised himself from the bed on the floor,
Drew on his war-dress, shirt, leggings, and girdled the
    belt around his waist,
Call'd for vermillion paint (his looking glass was held
    before him),
Painted half his face and neck, his wrists, and back-
    hands,
Put the scalp-knife carefully in his belt—then lying
    down, resting a moment,
Rose again, half-sitting, smiled, gave in silence his
    extended hand to each and all,
Sank faintly low to the floor (tightly grasping the
    tomahawk handle),
Fixed his look on wife and little children—the last: (And
    here a line in memory of his name and death).

COACOOCHEE, or WILD CAT: Coacoochee [ko-uh-KOO-chee] earned his war name of Wild Cat by his fierce resistance to the efforts of the United States to drive the Seminoles out of Florida. He was born in the Seminole village of Yulaka on the St. Johns River about 1816. He grew up with black people whose parents had been runaway slaves from Georgia or Alabama. When he became an important leader, bands of both blacks and Indians joined him.

In 1836 the Army captured Coacoochee's father and imprisoned him in the old fortress at St. Augustine. This was done to lure Coacoochee to the fort where the US agents wanted to talk with him about moving the Seminoles to territory in the west. Accompanied by a black companion, Wild Cat rode into the fort. He was wearing a colorful turban with a white plume in it, the sign of peace. But when he found out that the blacks in the tribe would not be allowed to go west, he refused to make a treaty. He told the white men that he considered the blacks his people and that they recognized him as their leader.

Later that year the Army persuaded Wild Cat and Osceola to come to St. Augustine again and to talk about peace. In spite of the flag of truce which they carried, Osceola and Wild Cat were taken prisoners and sent to Fort Moultrie in South Carolina. Osceola died there, but Wild Cat and his party of eighteen escaped. They ate nothing for six days so they could squeeze between the prison bars.

Back in Florida, Wild Cat became the great leader of the Seminole resistance. He was the US Army's "most wanted" Seminole. At last, in 1841, with his people starving and in rags, he surrendered to Lieutenant William Tecumseh Sherman, saying: "Why cannot we live here in peace? I could live in peace with [the white man], but they first steal our cattle and horses, cheat us, and take our lands. The white men are as thick as the leaves in the hammock; they come upon us thicker every year. They may shoot us, drive our women and children night and day; they may chain our hands and feet, but the red man's heart will always be free." With about two hundred others, he was sent west. "I was in hopes I would be killed in battle, but a bullet never reached me," he said

Billy Bowlegs
Wife of Billy Bowlegs.

After the death of Oscoela, Billy Bowlegs (above) became principal war chief. He continued the guerilla warfare, laying waste to large sections of the Florida frontier occupied by whites. His Indian name Bolek sounded like Bowlegs to the whites. His formal title was Halpuda Micco, meaning chief of the Alligator, or Halpuda, clan.

after he reached the Indian Territory.

When he died in 1857 Wild Cat was trying to develop a colony of Seminoles and free blacks in Mexico. He never wavered from his position that the blacks belonged in Seminole society. Without him, some of the black might have been returned to slavery.

# Sounds and Meanings

Seminole Place Names Used Today

Name and location	How to pronounce	What it means
Attapulgas Creek, Fla.	a-tah-PULL-gus	Dogwood grove.
Halpatiokee Swamp, Fla.	hal-pah-tih-OH-kee	Alligator water.
Hialeah, Fla.	high-ah-LEE-uh	Pretty prairie.
Hillolo, Fla.	hih-LOE-loe	Long-billed curlew.
Homosassa, Fla.	hoe-moe-SASS-uh	Where the wild pepper grows.
Itchepuckesassa River, Fla.	itch-eh-puck-eh-SASS-uh	Tobacco blossoms are there.
Loxahatchee, Fla.	lox-ah-HATCH-ee	Turtle river.
Oka Humpka, Fla.	oh-kah HUM-kuh	Lonely or bitter water.
Okaloosa, Fla.	oh-kah-LOO-suh	Black Water.
Okeechobee, Fla.	oh-kee-CHOE-bee	Big water.
Palatka, Fla.	puh-LAT-kuh	Boat crossing or ferry.
Pithlachascotee, Fla.	PITH-luh-chus-KOE-tee	Canoe cut. A place where canoes were made.
Tohopkee, Fla.	tuh-HOPE-kee	Fort.
Tsala Apopka Lake, Fla.	t'sal-uh uh-POPE-kuh	Trout eating place.
Wewahitchka Village, Fla.	we-wah-HITCH-kuh	Water eyes. Twin lakes near by resembled eyes.
Yahala, Fla.	yah-HAH-luh	Orange (the fruit).
Yeehaw, Fla.	yee-haw	Wolf.

A tattooed Timucua warrior carries a quiver full of poisoned arrows and a powerful bow more than six feet long.

9

Important
Small
Tribes

Timucuas

The Timucuas [tim-uh-KOO-uz] of Florida are remembered as the tribe that gave curious Europeans their first picture of native Americans. These were drawings and paintings done by Jacques Le Moyne, who came with a French expedition to north Florida in 1564. His assignment was to map the coast and to portray the natives. He made scores of drawings of life among the Timucuas: how they worshipped, how they made war, how they governed, how they celebrated marriages, how they planted, how they hunted alligators. A book of Le Moyne's works with his writings about the Timucuas was published in 1591 in Europe.

The Timucuas lived in the north half of Florida from the Suwanee River to the St. Johns. They were a tall, handsome people, noted for their heavily tattooed bodies. They lived in fortified villages surrounded by cornfields.

Life changed sharply for the Timucuas when the Spanish drove the French out of Fort Caroline in 1565. The Spanish wasted no time in trying to convert the Timucuas to Christianity. Indian villages became mission stations where Franciscan monks established schools and churches. From time to time the Timucuas rebelled against the missions, but such rebellions usually ended in death for those who opposed Spanish rule.

The Timucuas survived this strange way of life for a time. But their numbers slowly dwindled. Many died from the diseases brought by the Europeans. The final blow came from raids by the British and their Creek allies from the north. The Timucuas, who once had numbered 15,000, became a vanished tribe.

Natchez

Did white men ever encounter the mound builders? The question puzzles historians. We do know that French explorers in the Mississippi Valley found some people living much as the ancient mound builders had. These people were the Natchez Indians.

The Natchez were ruled by one calling himself the Great Sun, who traced his family back to the sun itself. In the tribe's social order, he was, of course, at the top—one of the Suns. At the bottom were the Stinkards.

Only the Great Sun's wife could share his meals. Any food that remained he pushed with his feet to the servants.

Outina, chief of the Timucuas, leads his warriors into battle. This drawing and many others were done from first hand observation by the Frenchman Jacques Le Moyne, who visited Florida in 1564

The king of the Natchez, called the Great Sun, traced his family back to the sun itself. His person was so sacred that his subjects carried him everywhere on a litter.

Wearing a crown of feathers, he was carried on a litter wherever he went. If he had to walk, Stinkards spread mats on the ground before him. When he died, his wife and all his Stinkard servants were strangled with bowstrings at his funeral. It was considered an honor to die with the Great Sun.

The Natchez lived in nine or more villages clustered a few miles from the Mississippi River near present-day Natchez, Mississippi. They numbered around 4,500 in the year 1650, the largest tribe on the lower Mississippi River.

After the French founded the colony of Louisiana in the early 1700s, the Natchez managed for a few years to live with white soldiers in their villages and white farmers tilling their land. Finally, provoked by abuses and killings, they rebelled and attacked the whites. The French, helped by the Choctaws, in turn almost wiped out the tribe in a bloody massacre in 1731. The Great Sun and his family were sold as slaves in Santo Domingo. A few survivors escaped and joined the Creeks, Chickasaws, and Cherokees. Among these tribes the Natchez gained a reputation as mystics, because they continued to practice their ancient religion.

When the Natchez moved west with the Creeks in 1836, only 300 of their number remained.

Alibamos and Koasatis

The Alibamo tribe gave its name to the river and in turn to the state of Alabama. *Alabama* comes from the Choctaw words meaning "Those who clear the land" or "thicket clearers."

Legend says that Alibamos first lived in Mexico. Then they crossed the Rio Grande and wandered east. For awhile they lived with the Choctaws. Still wandering eastward, they came to the river which bears their name. They broke away from the Choctaws and became one of the first tribes to join the Muscogees, in the alliance known as the Creek Confederacy.

Settling just below where the Coosa and Tallapoosa Rivers flow together to make the Alabama River, the Alibamos lived on the east side of the river in six towns. One of these

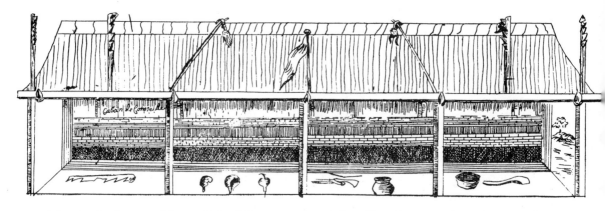

This sketch of a council house of the Alibamos was made by a Frenchman in the early 1700s. It shows medicine pots and spoons on the ground (right); gourd rattles and a conch shell dipper (left); a flag over the center pole; notched poles at each end; two poles carrying scalps (left and right of center); two full length cane seats. Note, under the roof at the left, the French words, Caban de Conseille (council house).

was Ikanatchati [ih-kahn-uh-CHAH-tee] (Red Ground), where Montgomery is today. De Soto visited another Alibamo town a short distance away, Tawasa, the site of Maxwell Air Force base.

The Alibamos were friendly with the French, who built Fort Toulouse in their area in 1717. But the French lost Fort Toulouse to the British in 1763; and because they did not like the British, many of the Alibamos moved away. Some followed the French to Louisiana and then on to Texas. Other bands settled among the Seminoles in Florida, or went with the Koasatis (see below) to the Tombigbee River. Some of the tribe, however, stayed among the Upper Creeks and fought in the Creek Indian War of 1813-14.

After the Creek Indian War the Alibamos were forced to leave their towns on the Alabama River. By 1832 they had only two towns left, Tawasa and Autauga. The people of these towns moved west to the new Indian Territory with other Creeks in 1836. Alibama Creek in Oklahoma bears their name.

The tribe called the Koasatis [koe-SAH-tees] were closely tied to the Alibamos. Like the Alibamos they joined the Creek Confederacy in the 1700s.

In 1540 De Soto found the Koasatis (Coste) living on an island, probably Pine Island, in the Tennessee River. By 1684 most of the tribe had moved down into Alabama and settled on the Alabama River. Their town, Koasati, was on the west bank of the river, opposite present-day Montgomery.

Shawnees

No other tribe seems to have divided so often or moved so frequently or roved so far as the Shawnees. They liked to make long treks, visiting, hunting, warring.

In the earliest times the Shawnees lived on the Ohio River. But war with the Iroquois forced them southward. In the South they first lived in two groups: one near Nashville, Tennessee, on the Cumberland River, another in South Carolina on the Savannah River. The Cherokees lived in between. As the English pushed in from the Atlantic coast and favored other tribes, the Shawnees had to leave. Some moved north, others settled in small bands as part of the Creek Confederacy in Alabama and Georgia.

The Shawnees lived easily with other tribes even though they kept their own identity. Few in number, they exerted

Tecumseh

much influence in whatever tribe they lived with. Having lived in many places, they knew firsthand the relentless push from all directions of white people onto Indian lands. They became leaders in spreading the doctrine of an Indian country for the Indians. As early as the 1750s emissaries from the Shawnees traveled widely among other tribes seeking support for one Indian federation allied against the whites.

The Shawnees' famous warrior-statesman, Tecumseh, visited the Southern tribes in 1811 trying to unify them against the United States. He spoke at Tukabachee, capital of the Creek Nation, where some 5,000 Creeks had gathered. He said: "Accursed be the race that has seized our country and made women of our warriors. Our fathers from their tombs reproach us as slaves and cowards. I hear them now in the wailing winds . . . Let the white race perish. They seize your land, they corrupt your women, they trample on the ashes of your dead. Back whence they came, upon a trail of blood, they must be driven."

Tecumseh's efforts were in vain. He was killed in battle, fighting the United States.

The Shawnees take their name from an Algonquian word meaning "south" or "southerners." The Creeks and the early white settlers called them Savannahs because they lived on the Savannah River in South Carolina and Georgia. The Shawnees call themselves Shawano. Their name in various forms lives on in place names throughout the South.

Catawbas

The name Catawba comes from two Yuchi words meaning "strong people." The Catawbas had taken under their protection lesser tribes such as the Waterees, Congarees, Santees, Waxhaws, Peedees, and Enos. They lived in the Piedmont area of South Carolina. The Catawbas are remembered as friends of the whites with whom they fought against the Cherokees.

The Catawbas and the Cherokees were always enemies. The story is told that when the Catawbas first came to the area of the Carolinas, the Cherokee blocked their way at the Catawba River. They fought a battle, but neither tribe won. They did agree that the Catawbas could live on the east side of the Broad River and the Cherokees on the west side. The area between was neutral territory. Stone piles were heaped on the battlefield to mark the treaty. Broad River after that was called Line River by the Catawbas.

The Catawbas were sometimes called Isswa, meaning "river people." They gave their name to the Catawba grape.

In early tribal days the Catawbas were good farmers and hunters. The women were noted as makers of pottery and basketry. They were the only people east of the Mississippi to use cylindrical strips of clay to make their pots.

Smallpox epidemics struck the Catawbas in 1759 and 1776 and, along with liquor, caused the once-powerful tribe to suffer a rapid decline. King Haiglar, best known of the Catawba chiefs, pleaded with Carolina officials not to give

In this old engraving Tecumseh kneels before his brother, called The Prophet. The two men visited the Southern tribes in their effort to unite all the Indian nations in opposing white takeover of Indian lands.

his people liquor: "It is very bad for our people, for it rots their guts and causes our men to get very sick. Many of our people have died by the effects of that strong drink."

Greatly beloved by his people, Haiglar was killed by Shawnees in 1763. In 1849, Samuel Scott, a grandson of Haiglar, signed a treaty giving more than 100,000 acres of fertile lands to the state of South Carolina for a few thousand dollars. The Catawbas were to move to North Carolina.

But North Carolina did not want the Catawbas, so they came back to South Carolina; 652 acres was the only land the tribe still had.

In 1848 the Catawbas asked the US Government to send them to Indian lands in the west. They wished to live with the Choctaws. In 1853 the Choctaws took in the Catawbas. Another group stayed in South Carolina, living on a state reservation on the Catawba River near Rock Hill. In 1970 only sixty members of the Catawba tribe still lived on this reservation. But by 1980 the tribe had found new life. The Catawbas now number 1,300 and are pressing their claim with Congress and the state for 140,000 acres of their ancestral homeland.

Yuchis

We first know about the Yuchis from De Soto, who found them living in east Tennessee. Later Europeans encountered them throughout the Southeast. The Yuchis moved often. They had towns in the areas of present-day South Carolina, Georgia, Alabama, and Florida. As the English pressed in from the Atlantic coast and the French from the Gulf, the Yuchis moved inland. Their main town spread for almost a mile on the west bank of the Chattahoochee River across from present-day Columbus, Georgia. The noted botanist William Bartram visited there in 1776 and described it as the "largest, most compact, and best situated Indian town" that he had seen. About 1,500 Yuchis lived there.

This large settlement owed its existence to a Creek chief of Cussita called Captain Allick. In 1729 he married a Yuchi woman and brought her back to Cussita. His marriage displeased the Creeks; so Captain Allick, with his three brothers, two of whom had also married Yuchi women, moved to the Chattahoochee River. He persuaded other bands of Yuchis to join them there.

Although a part of the Creek Confederacy, the Yuchis took pride in observing their own tribal customs and did not mix well in the confederacy. They called themselves "children of the sun." Many of their religious rituals centered around worship of the sun. They spoke only their Yuchi language and made no attempt to learn other dialects.

The Yuchis also looked different from most other Creeks. They were tall, light-skinned, and blue-eyed. The women were noted for their beauty and much sought after as wives.

Their independent ways angered other Creeks. Even so, they were welcomed as a strengthening force in the confederation, where they rapidly became a powerful influence.

The Yuchis went west during the Indian removal as a part of the Creeks, the first group with the Lower Creeks in 1829, the second with the main group of Creeks that left Alabama in 1836.

Descendants of these people meet once a year in Columbus, Georgia, and take part in tribal celebration.

Timpoochee Barnard, a Yuchi chief, fought with the Lower Creeks and Andrew Jackson in the Creek war of 1814. After the war he returned to his home on the Flint River in Georgia to live with his wife and six children.

TENNESSEE

NORTH
CAROLINA

SOUTH
CAROLINA

MISSISSIPPI

ALABAMA

GEORGIA

FLORIDA

10

Seeing
the South's
Indian Heritage

A Guide by States

In this section you can see the Southern Indians in the geographical bounds of seven states: Alabama, Florida, Georgia, Mississippi, North Carolina, South Carolina, Tennessee.

Who were the Indians who lived in each state before 1840? What Indian groups live there today? If the state's name is of Indian origin, what does it mean? These questions are answered under each state heading. More information about most of the tribal groups mentioned is found in other sections of the book.

Under each state heading you will also find a list of places to visit—museums, state parks, national monuments, archaeological sites which are open to the public—which provide glimpses of Indian history. Although most of the important places in each state are included, the listings may not cover all the sites which one may visit. For further information, check state tourist offices.

Scattered across these seven states are hundreds of Indian place names, beautiful in sound and interesting in meaning. A brief listing of such names—towns, counties, rivers, creeks—is provided in each of the chapters on tribes; see pages 67, 79, 99, 113, 125.

ALABAMA

The big bend of the Tennessee River flowing through north Alabama attracted the first Indians in the area. Here several archaeological discoveries have revealed important information about the state's earliest people.

A powerline worker chanced on ancient projectile (weapon) points near Russell Cave in 1953. Archaeologists came to investigate the find and uncovered the fact that Ice Age hunters had used the cave as long as 9,000 years ago.

Another major discovery about early Indians in Alabama was at the Quad site on the Tennessee River across from the city of Decatur. Digs there tell us that early peoples used this area for campsites. All kinds of tools—scrapers, knives, drills, choppers—along with projectile points, have been found there. Why did early man come here to camp? We think he came because of the animals feeding in the quiet backwaters of the river. The hunters could hide in the weeds and stalk the game.

A third important site of early man in Alabama is the Stanfield-Worley Bluff Shelter near Tuscumbia, also in the Tennessee Valley. In the 1960s Boy Scouts along with other volunteers joined archaeologists in a scientific dig. What they found showed that people had used this spot from earliest times to about A.D. 1500.

Other early Indians left their mark in a different way at Moundville on the Black Warrior River near Tuscaloosa. Here you can see the largest group of mounds in the Southeast, thirty-four of them, spread over an area of 305 acres. The people who lived here were known as master farmers and reached a high degree of civilization based on growing corn.

Four of the main southern Indian tribes lived in Alabama— the Chickasaws, Choctaws, Creeks, and Cherokees.

The Cherokees lived in the northeast corner of the state, the Chickasaws in the northwest, the Choctaws in the southwest, and the Creeks in the central and southeast areas. But these tribes lived in other states, too. Most of the Cherokees lived in Tennessee and North Carolina. The Chickasaws

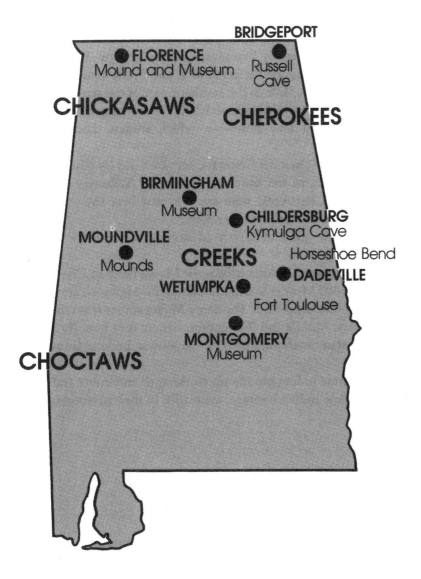

extended into north Mississippi and west Tennessee. The main body of the Choctaws lived in Mississippi.

The Creeks occupied more of Alabama than the other tribes. Their main settlements were along these rivers: the Coosa, Tallapoosa, Alabama, and Chattahoochee.

The name of the state comes from one of the Creek-related tribes, the Alibamos. The name means "Those who clear the land." It does not mean "Here were rest," as popularly believed.

In Alabama today live several Indian groups. The Poarch

Band of Creeks, also referred to as the Creek Nation East of the Mississippi, live in the southern part of the state near Atmore. They number about 1,300. Every year they hold a Thanksgiving Day Powwow, which attracts thousands of visitors.

About 600 Jackson County Cherokees, led by Chief Lindy Martin, live in the northeast corner of Alabama. Another group of Cherokees, who are scattered over the state, call themselves the Echota Cherokees.

The Star Clan of Lower Muscogee Creeks live in Pike County.

The largest Alabama tribe is the Mowa Band of Choctaws. Over 5,000 Mowas live in the Citronelle-McIntosh area close to the Mississippi line. The name Mowa comes from the two counties, Mobile and Washington, where they live. By an act of the state legislature in 1979 the Mowas became an official tribe.

All these Indian groups are working to rediscover and preserve their Indian heritage, especially in their native arts and crafts.

Seeing Alabama's Indian Heritage

BIRMINGHAM
Birmingham Museum of Art. Creek art and artifacts.
BRIDGEPORT
Russell Cave National Monument. This is prehistoric man's oldest known home in the South, dating from about 7,000 B.C. The cave, 107 feet wide, is made by a giant rock overhang. The floor of the cave goes far back from the opening; it provided shelter and a winter home, while in warm weather the Indians lived in the lowlands of the Tennessee River valley, a few mile below the cave. The museum ranger shows how to make a projectile point with the same tools the Indians used and demonstrates the use of the atlatl (spear-thrower).
CHILDERSBURG
Kymulga Cave (also called De Soto Caverns) is a large onyx

cave with prehistoric Indian burials. The cave is privately owned but open to the public for a small fee. Spanish relics have been found nearby. Near Childersburg was the Indian town of Coosa were De Soto camped for 25 days in 1540. Coosa was the capital of a large Indian territory with several thousand inhabitants.

DADEVILLE

Horseshoe Bend National Military Park. At the Battle of the Horseshoe in March 1814 one thousand Creek Indians under Chief Menawa died in a desperate effort to hold back Andrew Jackson's forces. As you walk around the battlefield you can stop at important points where tape recordings and diagrams tell the story of this important event in American history. Museum.

FLORENCE

Indian Mound and Museum. The largest mound on the Tennessee River, 43 feet high, with steps leading to the top. The museum contains displays of Indian artifacts.

MONTGOMERY

Department of Archives and History. Indian artifacts.

MOUNDVILLE

Moundville State Monument. One of the best-preserved prehistoric mound groups in the country. On the site are 34 mounds. Atop the restored temple mound is a life-size exhibit of an Indian religious ceremony. In the museum you can see the actual skeletal remains of 57 of these prehistoric people.

WETUMPKA

Fort Toulouse was built by the French in 1717 as an outpost for the fur trade with the Indians. on this spot where the Coosa and Tallapoosa Rivers join to form the Alabama River, there was once a village of the Alibamo tribe. Here the Creek leader William Weatherford (Red Eagle) signed a peace treaty with Andrew Jackson, ending the Creek Indian War in 1814. Working with the National Park Service, the Alabama Historical Commission is restoring the fort and excavating the area.

FLORIDA

Mound-building people have left their mark on Florida. A large group of burial mounds is preserved at Crystal River on the state's west coast. The temple mound at Fort Walton on the Gulf coast was once the religious ceremonial center for groups of mound builders living near by. They created fine ceremonial vessels in the likeness of animals.

Florida's Indians who came after the mound builders suffered more than any other Southern Indians at the hands of early European explorer and settlers. With the Atlantic Ocean on one side and the Gulf of Mexico on the other, natives of Florida had little chance to escape.

Three major tribes were on hand to meet the first white men. The Timucuas controlled north Florida. The Calusas ruled from Tampa south to the Everglades and through the Keys. The Apalachees claimed northwest Florida in the area of present-day Tallahassee. The Calusas and Timucuas rapidly became vanished tribes after white contact. A small number of Apalachees survived; they either left the state or joined the Seminoles.

Today the Seminoles are the tribe that we associate with Florida. They did not even exist as a tribe until the earlier tribes had disappeared. They live on five reservations in south Florida. (See pp. 120-21.)

Seeing Florida's Indian Heritage

BRADENTON
De Soto National Memorial commemorates De Soto's 1539 landing. On Terra Ceia Island is the *Madira Bickel Mound State Monument*, site of an Indian temple mound and the Indian village of Ucita where De Soto first camped.

BUSHNELL
Dade Battlefield State Historic Site and Museum. Seminoles attacked the whites here in 1835.

CRYSTAL RIVER
Crystal River State Archaeological Site. Fine group of Indian

burial mounds, trail-side displays, museum with Indian artifacts.

FORT WALTON BEACH

Temple Mound and Museum. One-acre mound served as a major religious and civic center for mound-building Indians. Dioramas, exhibits, artifacts.

HOLLYWOOD

Seminole Okalee Indian Village. Fourteen-acre village where Seminoles exhibit arts and crafts.

JACKSONVILLE

Fort Caroline National Monument. Sixteenth-century fort built by French and Spanish. Visitor center has large reproductions of Le Moyne drawings of Timucua Indians, and Timucua artifacts—beads, pottery, tools, effigies.

Jacksonville Children's Museum. Exhibits on archaeology and Indian life.

ORMOND BEACH

Tomoka State Park. Statue of Chief Tomoka stands where Tomoka River and Halifax River meet at site of old Indian village of Nocoroco. Museum.

PENSACOLA

Gulf Islands National Seashore—Fort Pickens area. Ruins of old Fort Pickens, where Geronimo (an Apache) was imprisoned.

Pensacola Historical Museum in restored Seville Square covers history of the area, from the time of prehistoric Indians.

T.T. Wentworth Jr. Museum. Florida relics and artifacts.

West Florida Museum of History. Gulf Coast History.

ST. AUGUSTINE

Castillo de San Marcos National Monument. Fort stands as evidence of the struggle of the Spanish and British for possession of Florida and the friendship of the Florida Indians. Wild Cat, the Seminole leader, led an escape from the fort.

GEORGIA

From shell heaps along the coast to cave shelters near Cartersville we find evidence of Georgia's first people.

But it is in central Georgia that we can see, all in one place,
the state's long Indian history. Probably more Indians used
the Okmulgee Old Fields at Macon over a longer period of
time than any other site we know about in the South. First
to come were the Ice Age hunters who camped here. Last
to come were the Creeks who built their town of Okmulgee on top of five levels of previous occupation. It is easy to
understand why Okmulgee National Monument ranks as
one of the important Indian sites in the US.

Another important Georgia landmark is Stallings Island,
near Augusta. The oldest pottery found in North America
came from Stallings Island. It dates back to about 2500
B.C.

At Sapelo Island on the coast below Savannah seven-
foot piles of shells form a circle more than 300 feet across.
We do not know how the Indians used the shell ring. It is
the largest of twenty shell mounds along the Georgia and
South Carolina coast. Many of Georgia's early people lived
along the Atlantic coast. The first white men found them
there living in small tribes. Some of the tribes died out, while
others moved away from the coast to inland Georgia and
joined other tribes to form the Creek Confederacy.

Best known of the coastal Indians were the Guales
[WAH-lees]. In early times their territory extended from St.
Andrews Sound to Savannah. Spanish missionaries settled
among them, and the Guales became the first Indians north
of Mexico to become Christians. A Spaniard, Domingo
Augustin, compiled a grammar of the Guale language, the
first for any Southern tribe. When Georgia became a British
colony the Guales fled with the Spaniards to Florida; only
a handful were left to join the Creek Confederacy.

Small but important tribes who lived along Georgia's
many rivers included the Hitchitis, Apalachees, Kashitas,
and Yuchis. They became part of the Creek Confederacy.
The Hitchitis claimed to be the oldest of the inland group;

ROSSVILLE
Ross House

CHATSWORTH
Vann House

CALHOUN
New Echota

CHEROKEES

CARTERSVILLE
Etowah Mounds

JACKSON
Indian Springs

EATONTON
Eagle Mound Effigy

CREEKS

MACON
Okmulgee

COLUMBUS
Museum

BLAKELY
Kolomoki Mounds

GUALES

they had lived at Okmulgee long before De Soto met them in 1540. (For more about the Yuchis, see p. 134.)

Two great tribes made up Georgia's Indian population in historic times: the Cherokees and the Creeks. The Cherokees lived in the northwest part of the state, spilling down from Tennessee and North Carolina. The Creeks lived over the rest of the state along the rivers. The Creeks were really many tribes who had joined together to make the Creek

Confederacy. In Georgia and east Alabama they were known as Lower Creeks. Their capital was at Coweta (across the river from Columbus).

So complete was the removal of the Creeks and Cherokees out of Georgia to the west in the 1830s that no reservations exist in Georgia today. A small group of Cherokees, however, lives in north Georgia, and another small group lives near Augusta.

Seeing Georgia's Indian Heritage

BLAKELY

Kolomoki Mounds State Park. Three mounds, 25-35 feet high and of an unusual conical shape, stand near Little Kolomoki Creek. Indians lived here a thousand years ago. Museum

CALHOUN

New Echota was the last capital of the Cherokee Nation in the East. A bronze tablet marks the site. The print shop of the newspaper *The Cherokee Phoenix*, published at New Echota, has been restored and reconstructed. A bronze statue of Sequoyah stands on the outskirts of the town.

CARTERSVILLE

Etowah Mounds Archaeological Area. Three large mounds mark this village site used from about A.D. 1000 to 1650. The largest of the mounds covers three acres, making it the second largest prehistoric mound in the US. (The largest is Cahokia in Illinois.) About 5,000 people lived on 52 acres surrounding the mounds. This was a social and religious center for the area. In the museum are two figures carved from white Georgia marble. The only prehistoric carvings from Georgia marble ever found, they probably took more than 100 years to carve and weigh over 130 pounds each.

CHATSWORTH

The Vann House, home of James Vann, who helped establish a school for young Cherokees, was the showplace of the Cherokee Nation.

COLUMBUS

Columbus Museum of Arts and Sciences. Display of Yuchi life and culture, artifacts.

EATONTON

Eagle Mound Effigy, called the most perfect effigy (shape of a figure) mound in the US, is more than 6,000 years old. The ten-foot-high mound of white quartz is shaped like a great bird with wings spread and its head turned eastward. It is 102 feet from head to tail and 120 feet from wingtip to wingtip.

JACKSON

Fifty miles southeast of Atlanta is *Indian Springs Museum and State Park.* The Creeks valued the mineral springs for their curative powers. The Creek chief William McIntosh built a cabin here; in 1825 he signed a treaty ceding much of Creek land to the whites.

MACON

Okmulgee National Monument was the first scientifically excavated Indian site in the South and has proved to be one of the most important sites in the US. Six different cultures lived here from 8000 B.C. to A.D. 1717. The largest temple mound stands 40 feet and contains about a million basket loads of earth. In a restored earthen lodge the visitor can see how the sacred fire was kept burning in a large sunken fire pit.

ROSSVILLE

The great Cherokee chief John Ross lived in a two-story log house, which still stands.

MISSISSIPPI

Through the years more Indians have lived in the area of present-day Mississippi than in any other Southern state.

The first Indians that we know of in Mississippi were the Mound Builders. Mounds and village sites are scattered all over the state. The Mound Builders were attracted to the area because of the mild climate, the many streams and rivers, and the broad, fertile valleys. It was an ideal location in which to settle down and raise corn.

In the area of the Mississippi River the Indians built flat-topped mounds that served either as burial mounds or as imposing bases for temples or chiefs' houses. At Winterville Mounds State Park at Greenville you can climb the temple mound, 55 feet high, and view the flat countryside for miles around. The Indians may have climbed on the tallest mound for safety when the great river flooded.

Near Robinsonville is the mound from which legend says De Soto in 1541 first glimpsed the Mississippi River. Not far away is a group of mounds marking the place where it is thought the Spanish explorer fought the Chisca (Chickasaws) and lost.

The most famous mound in Mississippi is Nanih Waiya, near present-day Noxapater, from which the Choctaws claim to have emerged. (See p. 152.)

By the year 1500, about the time the first white men arrived, many small but powerful tribes were living along the inland streams and rivers of Mississippi. The Chakchiumas, Ibitoupas, and Taposas lived on the upper Yazoo River; the Pascagoulas and the Acolapissas on the Pascagoula and Pearl Rivers; the Tunicas, Yazoos, Koroas, Tious, and Grigras on the lower Yazoo. These tribes disappeared quickly after their contact with white men. They either moved away, died out, or joined the Choctaws.

Another small tribe, the Biloxis, lived on the Gulf Coast. They helped the Frenchman Iberville establish a colony near the city which bears their name.

In the southwest corner of the state lived the Houmas, who gradually moved into Louisiana.

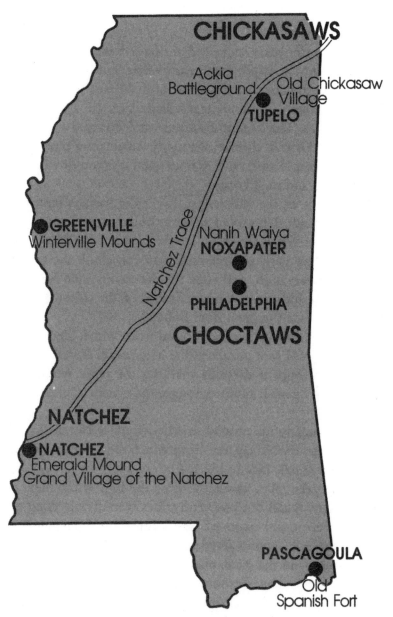

The three main tribes of Mississippi in later, or historic, times were the Choctaws, the Chickasaws, and the Natchez. The Chickasaws lived in the northern part of the state; their territory extended into Tennessee and Kentucky and the northwest tip of Alabama. The Natchez lived on the lower Mississippi River in a small area which is now Adams County. The Choctaws, the second largest tribe in the South (next to the Cherokees), spread over the south central part of the state and into Alabama. All the tribes had a common language: Muskogean.

By 1763 only the Chickasaws and the Choctaws still lived in Mississippi. The Natchez had been wiped out. The story of the Mississippi Indians after this date is one of retreat and loss.

In 1830 the Treaty of Dancing Rabbit Creek ended the Choctaw Nation in Mississippi. The Chickasaws signed away the last of their ancient homeland in 1832. About 5,000 Choctaws remained in Mississippi when the rest of the tribe moved west. Today about that same number live in east central Mississippi in and around Philadelphia. They are known as the Mississippi Band of Choctaw Indians. As far as we know, no Chickasaws stayed behind in Mississippi.

The state took its name from the river that forms its western border. The name is the white people's spelling of a simple Algonquian word, *misi sipi*, meaning "big water."

Seeing Mississippi's Indian Heritage

GREENVILLE
Winterville Mounds State Park and Museum (3 miles north of Greenville off State 1). Seventeen mounds, constructed between A.D. 1200 and 1400, make up one of the largest prehistoric Indian sites in the Mississippi Valley. Museum has displays of Indian life and archaeological artifacts.

NATCHEZ
Emerald Mound (off Natchez Trace on State 553). One of the largest Indian temple mounds in the US, built between A.D. 1300 and 1600 by forerunners of the Natchez. Climb to the top for a magnificent view.
Grand Village of the Natchez Indians. This site, center of Natchez Indian activity from 1682-1729, has been extensively restored, with a center housing artifacts and an auditorium where a film is presented.

NOXAPATER
Nanih Waiya (12 miles east of Noxapater on State 21). The

sacred site of the Choctaws was occupied from the time of Christ until the Europeans came. A large mound, a natural geological formation, is called "Great Mother" by the Choctaws, who believe it to be the birthplace of the tribe. Beneath the mound is a cave from which, legend says, the tribe emerged. A mile and a half to the west is a large, flat-topped, manmade mound, also a part of Choctaw tradition.

PASCAGOULA

Old Spanish Fort, possibly the oldest fortified building in the Mississippi Valley. Indian relics in museum.

PHILADELPHIA

Center of Mississippi's Indian country and headquarters of the Choctaw Indian Agency. Most of the Indians now in Mississippi live in the area. Choctaws hold an annual Indian Week, featuring arts and crafts displays, traditional Choctaw dress reviews and style shows, and competitions in stickball, blowgun, archery, drum-beating.

TUPELO

Ackia Battleground National Monument (between US 78 and State 6 on the old Natchez Trace). In 1736 the Battle of Ackia was fought on this site. The Chickasaws so badly defeated the expedition of Bienville, French governor of Louisiana, that he was forced to withdraw to Mobile, and France's position in the New World was permanently weakened.

Old Chickasaw Village (between US 78 and State 6) is the approximate location of a fortified Chickasaw village. Foundations of the fort and summer and winter houses have been marked. Exhibits interpret daily life of the Chickasaws.

Natchez Trace Parkway follows ancient Indian trails. Head-quarters and visitor center are 5 miles north of Tupelo. A museum room and audiovisual program tell the story of the Trace.

NORTH CAROLINA

In July 1916 two tropical storms met on the top of the Blue Ridge Mountains. The Yadkin and Catawba Rivers rose rapidly and swept down the valleys. Floods tore through many former Indian villages and campsites, exposing artifacts and skeletal remains. Here was evidence that hunters wandered through North Carolina more than 10,000 years ago. Clay pottery and polished stone pipes told of a later people who raised corn and built mounds. So we know North Carolina's Indian heritage reaches from earliest times to the present day.

The first contact between the area's Indians and Europeans (except for De Soto) took place along the Atlantic coast. Many small tribes lived in the coastal area. Soon after they met the white man they disappeared from history. Today their names live in place names.

Cape Fear bears the name of a group that was friendly to white settlers; they put to sea in canoes and rescued a British ship. Pamlico Sound carries the name of a tribe that was sold into slavery. Cape Hatteras, the site of many shipwrecks, was home to the Hatteras Indians, who lived on its sand banks.

The most important coastal tribe were the Tuscaroras. They fought the early white settlers and were defeated. Many Tuscaroras were sold into slavery. Those who were left moved to the Iroquois Indian League in New York state.

In the middle of the state, the Piedmont area, lived the Catawbas. Most of the Catawbas lived in South Carolina (see "South Carolina"). Smaller Piedmont tribes, such as the Cheraws, banded with the Catawbas for protection. The Cheraws are famous as the tribe that played host to De Soto for four days in 1540.

The Cherokees lived in the southwest tip of the Blue Ridge Mountain region of the state. They are the most famous tribe of North Carolina and one of the best known in the United States. Today about 5,000 Cherokees still live in on the reservation at Cherokee.

The Lumbees, who live mostly in Robeson County, largely

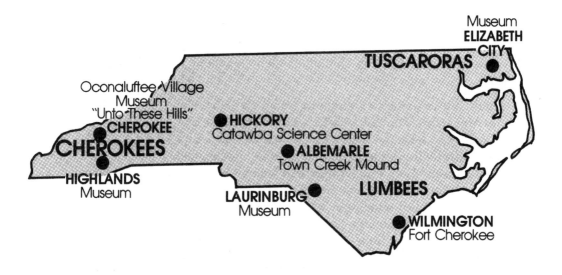

account for the surprising number of Indians who live today in North Carolina. In fact, they are the largest Indian group in the South, numbering about 30,000. Many people do not think of them as Indians because they have lost their native language and tribal customs. For 200 years the Lumbees lived like their white neighbors and spoke only English. Only the color of their skin made them different. Whites tended to group them with blacks, but the Lumbees want their own identity. They call themselves the Lumbee Indian tribe. They are not sure of their background, but some historians believe they are connected with the first English colony in America, established on Roanoke Island. The colony disappeared mysteriously between 1587 and 1590. The only clue was the name "Croatoan" carved on a tree. The Lumbees may be descendants of the Croatian Indians and the white colonists who joined them.

Today Indians of other tribes also live in the state, giving North Carolina a total Indian population of 44,000. Only Arizona, California, New Mexico, and Oklahoma have larger Indian populations.

Seeing N. Carolina's Indian Heritage

ALBEMARLE

Town Creek Indian Mound State Historic Site. Reconstructed sixteenth century Indian ceremonial center with stockade, temples, and mortuary.

CHEROKEE

Capital of the Eastern Band of the Cherokees, who live on the Qualla Reservation. These people are descendants of the Indians who hid in the mountains in the winter of 1838-39 to avoid being driven over the Trail of Tears to Oklahoma.

Oconaluftee Indian Village. Replica of Indian village of more than 200 years ago. Seven-sided council house. Lectures.

Museum of the Cherokee Indian. Arts and crafts, audiovisual displays, portraits, prehistoric artifacts.

"Unto These Hills." Outdoor drama recreating the history of the Cherokee Nation from 1540-1838.

Frontier Land. Recreated Indian village; Indian dances.

ELIZABETH CITY

Museum of the Albemarle. Indian exhibits.

HICKORY

Catawba Science Center. Indian exhibit.

HIGHLANDS

Museum of Natural History. Cherokee artifacts.

LAURINBURG

Indian Museum of the Carolinas. Extensive display of Indian artifacts from the region.

WILMINGTON

Fort Cherokee Trading Post. Indian artifacts and relics.

SOUTH CAROLINA

Mounds of sand and shell scattered along the state's coastline tell us that prehistoric people lived here, but they left no important sites. South Carolina is noted instead for being the home of at least 28 different tribes belonging to five different language families.

On the coastal plains, called the Low Country, the tribes were numerous and small. In the Up Country, or Piedmont area, they were few and large.

In the Low Country some twenty small tribes had banded together and become the Cusabas by the time the first whites arrived. These small tribes are remembered today in such place names as Edisto, Winyaw Bay, Isaw, Kiawah.

Never a strong group, the Cusabas tried to get along with the British colonists. Charleston, one of the oldest towns in the United States, was founded on land belonging to the Cusabas. But smallpox, war, and the practice of taking Indian slaves soon caused the Cusabas to die out.

The Cusabas and other Low Country Indians lived in constant fear of the Westo Indians, newcomers to the area who had settled on the Savannah River below Charleston. They were reported to be man-eaters. British colonists defeated the Westos in a deadly war about 1680. Only fifty Westos escaped to join the Creeks.

Up Country South Carolina was the home of the state's largest tribe, the Catawbas. They lived mainly in York and Lancaster Counties near the north border of the state and extended into North Carolina. (See p. 133.)

Seeing S. Carolina's Indian Heritage

CAMDEN
Weather vane at top of clock tower on Broad Street represents King Haiglar, chief of Catawba Indians, often called "patron saint of Camden."

CHARLESTON
Charleston Museum exhibits prehistoric Indian weapons

and artifacts.

COLUMBIA

University of South Carolina, McKissick Museum. Catawba
Indian pottery collection.

GREENVILLE

Greenville County Museum of Art. Indian artifacts.

GREENWOOD

The Museum. Indian artifacts.

Ninety Six National Historic Site. A village so named because
of its distance from Cherokee village of Keowee. Includes
Indian sites, remains of two historic villages.

PICKENS

Keowee–Toxaway State Park. Exhibits depict life and customs of Cherokees who lived in the area.

ROCK HILL

Catawba Indian Reservation. Several hundred Catawba
Indians still practice their ancient arts and crafts, such as
pottery and basket weaving.

TENNESSEE

Indians lived many thousands of years ago in what is now Tennessee. In the east, near the Tennessee River, a campsite of the Ice Age hunters has been found. It is known as the LeCroy site. Another important location of early peoples is at Eva near Camden—also on the Tennessee River but in the west. Called the Eva site, it attracted people who lived on fresh-water clams and hunted game in the nearby forests. They left behind shell mounds and all kinds of tools and weapon points.

Two groups of mound-building Indians in Tennessee are remembered for their handiwork. The Duck River Indians of middle Tennessee made beautiful flint-chipped objects such as sword-like blades, sun disks, and animal figures, all used in religious ceremonies. These people did not keep all of their handiwork at home; they traded long swords—some over two feet long—and other objects to other southern Indians, who wanted them for their ceremonials. In southeast Tennessee the Dallas Indians, named for the island they lived on, made shell ornaments of great beauty and used shell beads for leg bands and belts. Today Chickamauga Lake covers Dallas Island.

Another group of mound builders lived on Hiwassee Island, located where the Hiwassee and Tennessee Rivers flow together. Once this was an important center for the Temple Mound people. Their mounds and villages covered the 700-acre island from about A.D. 1100-1500.

Tennessee derives its name from Tenassee, an ancient town of the Cherokees. The Cherokees were the most important tribe to live in the area. The mountainous eastern region of the state (as well as adjoining areas of North Carolina, Georgia, and Alabama) was their homeland. They built their villages beside the many rivers that flowed through the mountains: the Tennessee, the Hiwassee, the Little Tennessee, the Ocoee. The Cherokee Nation centered in what is now Morgan County. Echota, the earliest Cherokee capital, was located there on the Little Tennessee River, 30 miles from present-day Knoxville. Nearby was Tellico Plains, a favorite

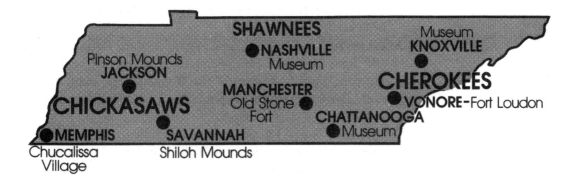

place for Cherokee ball games. The Cherokees who lived in Tennessee were known as the Over-the-Hill Cherokees.

Living in the west part of the state were the Chickasaws. Small in number, they had separated from the Choctaws to form their own tribe. The Chickasaws also occupied land in Mississippi and north Alabama. Chickasaw Bluff was probably on the site of present-day Memphis.

The Cherokees and the Chickasaws both claimed parts of middle Tennessee around Nashville, as did the Shawnees.

Seeing Tennessee's Indian Heritage

CHATTANOOGA

This city, former outpost of the Cherokees, was founded by John Ross, the great tribal chief. Chattanooga is near the starting point of the Trail of Tears, in which Indians from three states were herded by Federal troops and forced to march to Oklahoma.

Lookout Mountain Museum includes Indian artifacts.

JACKSON

Pinson Mounds Park. Remains of a large ceremonial center of the Temple Mound period, including 35 mounds, one of which is 73 feet high.

KNOXVILLE

University of Tennessee, Frank H. McClung Museum. Indian artifacts.

MANCHESTER

Old Stone Fort State Park. Remains of an ancient walled structure, built by Indians of the Woodland era, stand on bluffs above the forks of the Duck River. Museum. Library.

MEMPHIS

Chucalissa Indian Village. Restored thatched-roof houses, ceremonial plaza, temple mound, burial exhibits from about A.D. 900-1600.

NASHVILLE

Vanderbilt University, Kirkland Hall. Prehistoric Indian artifact collection, including terra cotta doll, modeled after a baby on a cradleboard, found in a child's grave; sandstone pipes, heads of which are in form of human heads with mouth open; sculpted heads, with look of portraits, used as mortuary vessels.

SAVANNAH

Shiloh Mounds, Shiloh National Military Park.

VONORE

Fort Loudon. Restored palisade fort. Rebuilt powder magazine. Museum. The western outpost of the British during French and Indian War was besieged by Cherokees in 1760.

Highlights of Southern Indian History

Important Dates of the Historic Period, 1513–1840

1513   First meeting between Southern Indians and Europeans occurs when Ponce de Leon (Spanish) explores Florida coasts, encountering Calusas and Timucuas.

Beginning of 300-year effort of Spain to claim the New World.

1521   Lucas Azquez de Ayllon (Spanish) explores Winyaw Bay (South Carolina) and sails off with Indians as captives.

1528   Indians of west Florida oppose efforts of Panfilo de Narvaez (Spanish) to conquer them and establish a Spanish colony.

1539–42 Hernando De Soto lands at Tampa Bay; explores the Southern inland; meets many different groups of Indians, devastating most of those in his path.

1559–61 Tristan de Luna (Spanish) lands at Pensacola Bay (Florida) with a large expedition; attempts, unsuccessfully, to found a Spanish colony.

1564   Jacques Le Moyne (French) paints and draws

A Calusa Indian carved this deer head, above, of wood and attached the ears so they could be moved by strings. In addition to being used in ceremonies, the head probably served as a lure for game. Buried for more than five hundred years in the mud bogs of Key Marco, Florida, it is one of the finest pieces of early Indian art in the country.

Landing in Florida, Ponce de Leon's men use guns and dogs against Indians.

life among Florida Indians, giving curious Europeans their first view of native Americans.

1565–67   Under Pedro Menendez de Aviles, Spanish found St. Augustine on Timucuan land (Fla.); oust French from area.

1567–72   French, with aid of Indians, take parts of Florida from Spanish; try to convert Indians to Christianity.

1576   Spanish, under Pedro Menendez Marques, retake part of Florida, capturing and killing many Indians.

1577–1655   Spanish undertake strong missionary efforts among Florida Indians, with little success.

1629   British takeover of Indian land in the Carolinas begins. Small coastal tribes are the first to lose their land. British trade with Indians (mostly Creeks and Chickasaws) flourishes, mainly in deerskins and Indian slaves.

1670   British found Charleston (South Carolina).

1671–83   Indians of the Carolinas fight the British. Westos are almost wiped out.

1690   British enter Cherokee country.

1698   Chickasaws make contact with British for the first time.

1698–1702   French settle Mississippi Valley, build forts on Biloxi Bay and Mobile River.

1704	British, with Indian allies, move through South Carolina, Georgia, and into Florida, killing and enslaving Guales, Apalachees, Timucuas, Calusas.
1711–12	Tuscaroras of North Carolina battle colonists but are defeated; leave South and join Iroquoian League.
1715–17	Yamassees and Creeks revolt against slave trade but are defeated by whites in struggle for control of Carolinas.
1717–29	French expand their control of Mississippi Valley into Choctaw and Chickasaw country; found New Orleans; build Fort Toulouse (Ala.).
1721	South Carolina becomes a British colony.
1729	Chickasaws, Natchez, Yazoos attack French settlements in Mississippi Valley.
	North Carolina becomes a British colony.
1731	Natchez tribe is wiped out in massacre by French and Choctaws.
1733	Creek chief Tomochichi greets James Oglethorpe at Yamacraw Bluff. Oglethorpe founds Savannah. Loss of Creek land begins.
1735	French build Fort Tombecbe on Tombigbee River in Choctaw country (near present-day Epes, Ala.).
1736	In Battle of Ackia (near present-day Tupelo, Miss.) Chickasaws defeat French.
1739	Oglethorpe maintains peace with Creeks in Georgia.
1754	Georgia becomes a British colony.
1754–61	British struggle with French for control of Cherokee country.
1759, 1776	Smallpox epidemics ravage Cherokees and Catawbas.

Creek chief Tomochichi, shown here with his nephew Toonabey, in 1734 went to London with James Oglethorpe to sign a peace treaty.

Indians raid a pioneer settlement.

1763	Attakullakulla (Cherokee) and other Southern chiefs make peace treaty with British.
	French give up all their holdings in North America, including Fort Toulouse.
1765	Choctaws cede to Britain a large chunk of their land.
1773–77	William Bartram, naturalist, journeys through South, visiting Indian towns along the way.
1775	James Adair, British trader to the Southern tribes, publishes his history of Southern Indians in London.
1780	Spanish rebuild Fort Tombecbe in Choctaw country, calling it Fort Confederation.
1786	Chickasaws make their first treaty with the US, at Muscle Shoals.
	First treaty between Choctaws and US, signed at Hopewell, South Carolina, promises protection to the tribe in return for land.
1801	Chickasaws lose to US their right of way on Natchez Trace. In Treaty of Fort Adams, Choctaws give up land on Mississippi River.
1802	Choctaws lose more of their land in Alabama.
1805	Five million more acres of Choctaw land in

Alabama are ceded by that tribe in Treaty of Mt. Dexter.

1811   Tecumseh, Shawnee chief, visits Southern tribes to rally support for Indian unity.

1812   US Army enters Seminole country to keep Indians from joining British.

1813   Hostilities between Creeks and whites in Alabama are touched off by Battle of Burnt Corn, the massacre at Fort Mims, and Battle of Holy Ground.

1813–14   Creek Indian War.

1814   US forces, under Andrew Jackson and aided by Cherokees and Lower Creeks, defeat Upper Creeks at Battle of Horseshoe Bend (Ala.). Creeks cede to US nearly half of present state of Alabama. Fort Jackson is erected on site of Fort Toulouse.

1815   Chickasaws help General Jackson in Battle of New Orleans.

1816   Chickasaws give up claim to territory south of Tennessee. Choctaws sign treaty relinquishing rest of their land east of Tombigbee River.

First Seminole War begins.

1817   Alabama Territory created.

1818   At Treaty Ground of Old Town, Chickasaws give up more of their land.

1820   Choctaws cede further land in Doak's Stand Treaty.

1821   Sequoyah completed system for written Cherokee language.

US buys Florida from Spain and claims Seminole lands.

1823   Seminoles are forced to give up 32 million acres.

1825   McIntosh signs Treaty of Indian Springs on behalf of Creeks.

Paddy Carr, a Creek, accompanied Opothle-Yaholo to Washington in 1826. He sat for this portrait while on that mission.

Chittee-Yoholo, a Seminole war chief, was, according to Indian agent Thomas McKenney, a "superb guerrilla fighter, a night raider who slipped in and out of swamps to attack outposts."

1826	Menawa, in Washington, D.C., signs a new treaty for Creeks.
1827	Cherokees form a system of government modeled on that of the United States.
	The Cherokee Phoenix, Cherokee newspaper, begins publication at New Echota, Georgia.
1828	First group of (Lower) Creeks is moved out of Alabama for resettlement in Oklahoma.
1830	President Andrew Jackson signs Indian Removal Act authorizing him to resettle Indians east of Mississippi River in new lands west of Mississippi River. Choctaws sign Treaty of Dancing Rabbit Creek, losing last of their lands.
1831–33	Choctaws are moved from Mississippi to Indian Territory.
1832	By Treaty of Pontotoc, Chickasaws give up last of their land. Creeks cede to US last of their land. In Payne's Landing Treaty, Seminoles lose all their land.
1835	Major Ridge signs Treaty of New Echota on behalf of Cherokees.
1835–43	Second Seminole War.
1836	Last group of Creeks is moved out of Alabama.
1836–37	Chickasaws make removal trek to Oklahoma.
1838	Trail of Tears, Cherokees' removal to Oklahoma, begins.
1840	Catawbas lose most of their land in South Carolina.
	Removal of other tribes is complete.

References and Recommended Reading

Of the many printed sources used in preparing this book, those listed below were most helpful. Books marked * are especially recommended for young people who wish to pursue further their interest in the Southern Indians.

*Akens, Helen Morgan, and Brown, Virginia Pounds. *Alabama Mounds to Missiles.* Rev, ed. Huntsville, Ala.: Strode Publishers, 1972.

Armstrong, Virginia Irving, comp. *I Have Spoken: American History Through the Voices of the Indians.* Chicago: The Swallow Press, 1971.

*Baldwin, Gordon C. *How Indians Really Lived.* New York: G.P. Putnam, 1967.

*Brown, Virginia Pounds. *The Gold Disc of Coosa.* Huntsville, Ala.: Strode Publishers, 1975.

Brown, Virginia Pounds, and Akens, Helen Morgan. *Alabama Heritage.* Huntsville, Ala.: Strode Publishers, 1967.

*Burt, Jesse, and Ferguson, Robert B. *Indians of the Southeast: Then and Now.* Nashville: Abingdon Press, 1973.

Corkran, David H. *The Creek Frontier 1540-1783.* Norman: University of Oklahoma Press, 1967.

Cotterrill, R.S. *The Southern Indians: The Story of the Civilized Tribes Before Removal.* Norman: University of Oklahoma Press, 1954.

De la Vega, Garcilaso. *The Florida of the Inca.* Edited by John Grier Varner and Jeannette Johnson Varner. Austin: University of Texas Press, 1951.

Debo, Angie. *The Rise and Fall of the Choctaw Republic.* 2d ed. Norman: University of Oklahoma Press, 1967.

*Dockstader, Frederick J. *Great North American Indians: Profiles in Life and Leadership.* New York: Van Nostrand Reinhold Co., 1977.

Federal Writers' Project of the Works Progress Administration. *Florida: A Guide to the Southernmost State.* American Guide Series. New York: Oxford University Press, 1939.

_____. *Georgia: A Guide to Its Towns and Countryside.* American Guide Series. Athens: University of Georgia Press, 1939.

_____. *Mississippi: A Guide to the Magnolia State.* American Guide Series. New York: Viking Press, 1938.

_____. *North Carolina.* American Guide Series. Chapel Hill: University of North

Carolina Press, 1939.

_____. *South Carolina: A Guide to the Palmetto State.* American Guide Series. New York: Oxford University Press, 1941.

_____. *Tennessee A Guide to the State.* American Guide Series. New York: Viking Press, 1939.

Fundaburk, Emma Lila, ed. *Southeastern Indians: Life Portraits, a Catalogue of Pictures 1564-1860.* Luverne, Ala.: Emma Lila Fundaburk, 1958.

Fundaburk, Emma Lila. *Sun Circles and Human Hands: the Southeastern Indians.* Luverne, Ala.: Emma Lila Fundaburk, 1957.

*Gridley, Marion. *American Indian Women.* New York: Hawthorn, 1974.

*Gridley, Marion. *Indian Tribes of America.* Northbrook, Ill.: Hubbard Press, 1973.

*Gridley, Marion E. *The Story of the Seminole.* Indian Nation Series. New York: G.P. Putnam, 1973.

Hamilton, Virginia Van der Veer. *Seeing Historic Alabama: Fifteen Guided Tours.* University: University of Alabama Press, 1982.

*Hamilton, Virginia Van der Veer. *The Story of Alabama.* Montgomery, Ala.: Viewpoint Publications, 1980.

Harper, Frances, ed. *Travels of William Bartram.* New Haven: Yale University Press, 1958.

Hassrick, Royal B. *The George Catlin Book of American Indians.* New ed. New York: Promontory Press, 1981.

Hawkins, Benjamin. *The Creek Country.* Americus, Ga.: Americus Book Co., 1938.

*Horan, James D. *The McKenney-Hall Portrait Gallery of American Indians.* New York: Crown Publishers, 1972.

Hudson, Charles. *The Southeastern Indians.* Knoxville: University of Tennessee Press, 1976.

*Jacobson, Daniel. *Great Indian Tribes.* Maplewood, N.J.: Hammond, 1970.

Jahoda, Gloria. *The Trail of Tears.* New York: Holt, Rinehart and Winston, 1975.

Josephy, Alvin M., Jr., ed. *The American Heritage Book of Indians.* American Heritage Publishing Co., 1961.

Josephy, Alvin M., Jr. *The Indian Heritage of America.* New York: Alfred A. Knopf, 1968.

Lewis, Thomas M. N., and Kneberg, Madeline. *Tribes That Slumber: Indians of the Tennessee Region.* Knoxville: University of Tennessee Press, 1958.

Lorant, Stefan, ed. *The New World, First Pictures of America.* Rev. ed. New York: Duell, Sloane and Pearce, 1965.

McCracken, Harold. *George Catlin and the Old Frontier.* New York: Dial Press, 1959.

*McSpadden, J. Walker. *Indian Heroes.* New York: Thomas Y. Crowell, 1928.

*Moyer, John W. *famous Indian Chiefs.* Chicago: M. A. Donahue, 1957.

Myron, Robert. *Mounds, Towns and Totems: Indians of North America.* Cleveland: World, 1966.

National Geographic Society. *Indians of the Americas.* Washington, D.C.: National Geographic Society, 1955.

_____. *World of the American Indian.* Washington, D.C.: National Geographic Society, 1964.

*Reader's Digest. *America's Fascinating Indian Heritage.* Pleasantville, N.Y.: Reader's Digest, 1978.

Pickett, Albert James. *History of Alabama and Incidentally of Georgia and Mississippi from the Earliest Period.* Annals of Alabama 1819-1900 by Thomas McAdory Owen. Birmingham, Ala.: Webb Book Co., 1900.

Rights, Douglas L. *The American Indian in North Carolina.* Winston-Salem: John F. Blair, Publishers, 1957.

Satz, Ronald N. *Tennessee's Indian Peoples from White Contact to Removal, 1540–1840.* Knoxville: University of Tennessee Press, 1979.

Smith, Buckingham, trans. *Narratives of De Soto.* Gainesville, Fla.: Palmetto Books, 1968.

*Steele, William O. *The Wilderness Tattoo.* New York: Harcourt Brace, 1972.

Swanton, John R. *The Indian Tribes of North America.* Washington, D.C.: Smithsonian Institution, 1952.

_____. *The Indians of the Southeastern United States.* Washington, D.C.: US Government Printing Office, 1946.

*Tamarin, Alfred. *We Have Not Vanished: Eastern Indians of the United States.* Chicago: Follett, 1974.

*Tunis, John. *Indians.* Rev. ed. New York: Cromwell, 1979.

Walker, Alyce Billings, ed. *Alabama: A Guide to the Deep South.* New rev. ed. Originally compiled by the Federal Writers' Project of the Works Progress Administration. American Guide Series. New York: Hastings House, 1975.

Walthall, John A. *Prehistoric Indians of the Southeast: Archaeology of Alabama and the Middle South.* Tuscaloosa: University of Alabama Press, 1980.

Williams, Samuel C., ed. *Adair's History of the American Indians.* Johnson City, Tenn.: Watauga Press, 1930.

*Wimberly, Christine Adcock. *Exploring Prehistoric Alabama Through Archaeology.* Birmingham, Ala.: Explorer Books, 1980.

Wright, Muriel H. *A Guide to the Indian Tribes of Oklahoma.* Norman: University of Oklahoma Press, 1951.

Credits

Page 18: Natural Museum of Anthropology, Mexico City. Pages 24, 89: National Park Service, US Department of Inrerior. Page 24: Alabama Archaeology Society. Page 31: Birmingham (Ala.) Chamber of Commerce. Page 30: Museum of the American Indian, Heye Foundation. Pages 34, 48, 49, 50, 55, 63, 74, 91, 93, 96, 102, 104, 108, 111, 114, 118, 124, 128, 130, 135, 163, 164: Bureau of American Ethnology, Smithsonian Institution. Pages 32, 133: Library of Congress. Pages 36–37: Schoolcraft, *Indian Tribes of the United States.* Pages 40–41: Bureau of Publicity and Information, State of Alabama. Pages 46, 121: National Anthropological Archives, Smithsonian Institution. Page 54: Kaye Carlisle. Page 56: Iva Jewel Tucker. Pages 107, 119, 120: Home Mission Board, Southern Baptist Convention. Page 89: Robert Graves Studio. Pages 95, 97: Alabama Department of Archives and History. Page 98: Poarch Band of Creeks, Creek Nation East of the Mississippi. Page 123: Walt Whitman, *Leaves of Grass,* ed. Malcolm Cowley (New York: Funk and Wagnalls, 1968), p. 463. Page 126: The British Museum. Page 163: Office of Anthropology, Smithsonian Institution. Page 165: University Museum, Philadelphia.

Index

Page numbers in bold type indicate illustrations, maps, and captions.